A MATTER OF LIFE AND DEATH

IMMIGRANT COMMUNITIES & ETHNIC MINORITIES IN THE UNITED STATES & CANADA: No. 52

ISSN 0749-5951

Series Editor: Robert J. Theodoratus
Department of Anthropology, Colorado State University

1. James G. Chadney. *The Sikhs of Vancouver.*
2. Paul Driben. *We Are Metis: The Ethnography of a Halfbreed Community in Northern Alberta.*
3. A. Michael Colfer. *Morality, Kindred, and Ethnic Boundary: A Study of the Oregon Old Believers.*
4. Nanciellen Davis. *Ethnicity and Ethnic Group Persistance in an Acadian Village in Maritime Canada.*
5. Juli Ellen Skansie. *Death Is for All: Death and Death-Related Beliefs of Rural Spanish-Americans.*
6. Robert Mark Kamen. *Growing Up Hasidic: Education and Socialization in the Bobover Hasidic Community.*
7. Liucija Baskauskas. *An Urban Enclave: Lithuanian Refugees in Los Angeles.*
8. Manuel Alers-Montalvo. *The Puerto Rican Migrants of New York City.*
9. Wayne Wheeler. *An Analysis of Social Change in a Swedish-Immigrant Community: The Case of Lindsborg, Kansas.*
10. Edwin B. Almirol. *Ethnic Identity and Social Negotiation: A Study of a Filipino Community in California.*
11. Stanford Neil Gerber. *Russkoya Celo: The Ethnography of a Russian-American Community.*
12. Peter Paul Jonitis. *The Acculturation of the Lithuanians of Chester, Pennsylvania.*
13. Irene Isabel Blea. *Bessemer: A Sociological Perspective of a Chicano Bario.*
14. Dorothy Ann Gilbert. *Recent Portuguese Immigrants to Fall River, Massachusetts: An Analysis of Relative Economic Success.*
15. Jeffrey Lynn Eighmy. *Mennonite Architecture: Diachronic Evidence for Rapid Diffusion in Rural Communities.*
16. Elizabeth Kathleen Briody. *Household Labor Patterns among Mexican Americans in South Texas: Buscando Trabajo Seguro.*
17. Karen L. S. Muir. *The Strongest Part of the Family: A Study of Lao Refugee Women in Columbus, Ohio.*
18. Judith A. Nagate. *Continuity and Change Among the Old Order Amish of Illinois.*
19. Mary G. Harris. *Cholas: Latino Girls and Gangs.*
20. Rebecca B. Aiken. *Montreal Chinese Property Ownership and Occupational Change, 1881—1981.*
21. Peter Vasiliadis. *Dangerous Truths: Interethnic Competition in a Northeastern Ontario Goldmining Community.*
22. Bruce La Brack. *The Sikhs of Northern California, 1904—1975: A Socio—Historical Study.*
23. Jenny K. Phillips. *Symbol, Myth, and Rhetoric: The Politics of Culture in an Armenian-American Population.*
24. Stacy G. H. Yap. *Gather Your Strength, Sisters: The Emerging Role of Chinese Women Community Workers.*
25. Phyllis Cancilla Martinelli. *Ethnicity In The Sunbelt: Italian-American Migrants in Scottsdale, Arizona.*
26. Dennis L. Nagi. *The Albanian-American Odyssey: A Pilot Study of the Albanian Community of Boston, Massachusetts.*
27. Shirley Ewart. *Cornish Mining Families of Grass Valley, California.*
28. Marilyn Preheim Rose. *On the Move: A Study of Migration and Ethnic Persistence among Mennonites from East Freeman, South Dakota.*
29. Richard H. Thompson. *Toronto's Chinatown: The Changing Social Organization of an Ethnic Community.*
30. Bernard Wong. *Patronage, Brokerage, Entrepreneurship and the Chinese Community of New York.*

A MATTER OF LIFE AND DEATH

HEALTH-SEEKING BEHAVIOR OF GUATEMALAN REFUGEES IN SOUTH FLORIDA

Maria Andrea Miralles

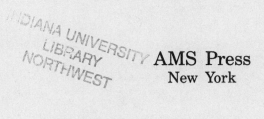

AMS Press
New York

Library of Congress Cataloging-in-Publication Data

Miralles, Maria Andrea.
    A matter of life and death : health-seeking behavior of Guatemalan
refugees in South Florida / by Maria Andrea Miralles.
    p. cm. — (Immigrant communities & ethnic minorities in the
United States & Canada ; 52)
Bibliography: p.
Includes index.
ISBN 0-404-19462-1
    1. Health behavior—Florida.   2. Kanjobal Indians—Health and
hygiene.   3. Indians of North America—Florida—Health and
hygiene.
4. Indians of Central America—Guatemala—Health and hygiene.
5. Refugees—Guatemala—Health and hygiene.   6. Refugees—
Florida—Health and hygiene.   I. Title.   II. Series.
RA448.5.I5M57   1989
362.1'08997—dc19   88-36497
                                                                        CIP

All AMS books are printed on acid-free paper that meets
the guidelines for performance and durability of the Committee on Production Guidelines for Book Longevity of the
Council on Library Resources.

AMS PRESS
56 East 13th Street
New York, N.Y. 10003, U.S.A.

MANUFACTURED IN THE UNITED STATES OF AMERICA

TABLE OF CONTENTS

LIST OF TABLES

LIST OF FIGURES

ACKNOWLEDGEMENTS

This book is based on my thesis for the Master of
Arts degree in anthropology from the University of
Florida, completed in December, 1986. Thanks to many
caring individuals, moral support and encouragement
throughout my studies were never lacking, especially
when most needed. Special mention is due to my parents,
Oma, brothers and sisters, and to friends and colleagues
in "the basement" too numerous to name.

A great debt of gratitude is due to the Holy Cross
Catholic Church and Service Center workers in
Indiantown, the Martin County Health Department,
Indiantown Unit, and the Florida Community Health
Center. Their concern, consideration and support
prompted me to take on and continue this project. I am
grateful for the willingness with which they accepted
this budding anthropologist into their busy lives in the
belief that something good would come of it.

Of course, none of this research would have been
possible without the kindness of the Kanjobal refugees
who allowed me an insight to their turbulent and

frequently troubled lives and still put up with my endless questions. I dedicate this book to the men, women and children of San Miguel Acatan who have taught me a great lesson in courage and faith. I hope that this study marks only the beginning of many to come that will help us all to understand the lives of refugees here and elsewhere, to protect refugee rights, and to help them meet their needs and carry on.

The successful completion of this research would not have been possible without the guidance and wisdom of my committee members, Drs. Allan Burns and Otto von Mering from the University of Florida Department of Anthropology, and Dr. Judy Perkin, Director of the Clinical and Community Dietetics program. Also deserving special mention is anthropologist Dr. Leslie Sue Lieberman. Their combined expertise and talents stimulated me throughout my graduate studies.

Finally, credit must be given to the patience, understanding and good humor of my husband, Glaucio, and to Sergei, Alexei, Yuri and Andrei who put up with my erratic lifestyle throughout the research, writing and production phases.

Maria A. Miralles
Gainesville, Florida

PREFACE

One afternoon I received a telephone call from a nurse at the university hospital. A newborn baby had just had a heart operation and the hospital staff was not able to communicate with the mother. She was Latin American, but apparently did not speak Spanish. When I arrived at the intensive care unit I saw a list of last names next to a set of monitors. One baby was simply "Baby Andres." Inside the intensive care area I was taken to see a mother and a baby - the baby was sedated as he was connected to several monitoring devices and bandaged over his small chest. The mother looked very frightened. I asked in Spanish, "are you from Indiantown?" "Yes," she answered quickly. "Do you know Maria Miralles?" I asked. "Yes," she answered with a slight smile.

Maria had been living in Indiantown studying issues of refugee community health. This afternoon she too had been called. When Maria came into the hospital room a few minutes later, the woman smiled again and began talking with her about the baby. "Marta," the woman who had come from Indiantown, was a Kanjobal Mayan who had taken an eight hour bus trip up to Gainesville to be with her baby as it

underwent an emergency heart operation. While she spoke
Spanish, it was Mayan Spanish of Guatemala. She did not
feel comfortable answering the nurses and doctors of the
hospital who tried out the few words and phrases they knew
in Spanish. Marta dealt with the unfamiliarity of the
setting and fear for her baby's life with silence.

The operating physician and the attending nurses
explained how the baby would have to be treated very
carefully for the next several months with special
medications, constant home care, and several return visits
to the hospital. Maria carefully explained all of this to
Marta, and when she was done, Marta looked up and said
simply, "My baby is going to die, isn't he?" Maria
translated this concern to the nurse and the doctor who
reassured her that the baby would be fine with proper care.
What Marta, Maria and I knew, though, was that living
conditions in Indiantown for Kanjobal Mayan refugees from
Guatemala were far from ideal for the kind of care that the
baby would require. We were all silent for a few minutes.

Small towns in the United States are often thought of
in terms of ideal rural communities with mainstreet
simplicity, friendly neighbors, and patterns of culture
recognizable to us all. Indiantown, Florida is a small town
of little more than three thousand people, but it is not

part of the small town America of popular belief. It is a community of diversity and vibrancy and sometimes of conflict. It is a community where people find tremendous diversity. The community boasts a retirement image like many small towns in the sun belt; luxury yachts are parked along the intercoastal waterway that leads to the Atlantic ocean, lots are sold on a local golf course. But the community is also a town of migrant workers, many living three or four families to an apartment. It is a town with great ethnic diversity: Mexicans, Central Americans, people from the Caribbean, American Blacks live side by side with Whites. Indiantown is not the community portrayed in theme parks or on television.

At the end of 1982, Indiantown became the home of a few Kanjobal Mayan refugees who were brought to Florida by a crew boss from a migrant camp. The Kanjobal people came from rural hamlets in the Northwestern highlands of Guatemala. They had escaped with little more than their lives from the civil war and violence of the area. Indiantown, as "El Pueblo de los Indios," became a goal for other Kanjobal Maya people escaping the terrorism of their homeland. In a few short years Indiantown gained a significant population of Mayan people.

The Kanjobal people came as families. Women and men whose spouses had been killed came with their children and other relatives to Indiantown and set up households. The households were different from what they had known in Guatemala. In the mountains cool, thin air demanded the houses be dark and closed. Villages were dispersed in the highlands and people in small hamlets of twenty to fifty people met when they went to town on market days. In Indiantown people live together crowded into the few available houses and apartments that can be found. In Guatemala health was gained by hard work, living within the values of Kanjobal religious life, and by seeking out western or indigenous medical help when necessary. Indiantown, on the other hand, is in the United States. Many health options are available to people, ranging from local and county clinics to regional hospitals fully equipped with the latest of modern medical technology. Health care is costly, however, especially for the Kanjobal refugees who do not have legal status in this country. In addition, health care workers and medical personnel in Indiantown were not familiar with either the history of the Kanjobal people of their language, one of the more than twenty-five Mayan languages spoken in Guatemala and Mexico.

PREFACE
_____

Maria Miralles worked in Indiantown as a health
assistant, as a friend to many Kanjobal people, and as an
applied anthropologist. Her goal was to work with different
institutions: local health clinics, offices of social
service agencies, legal assistance agencies, and churches
that help migrant workers. Instead of attaching herself to
one office and becoming identified in just one context,
Maria developed a role for herself as a fieldworker able to
assist with many agencies. But Maria was able to use her
diffuse role to be effective in the midst of these
conflicts. Her ability to work with many groups extended to
informal settings as well. When Kanjobal people became
envied because of the special treatment they seemed to
receive, Maria worked to maintain contact with other
hispanic and non-hispanic populations of the town.

The difficulty of working on topics such as health in a
community setting is that the problems swirl into a vortex
of social and cultural conditions. Farmwork is dangerous
for people not accustomed to pesticides, climbing ladders,
or crowded quarters. Kanjobal people think and speak in a
different language; translations from English through
Spanish into Kanjobal are subject to misinterpretations.
Kanjobal refugees are considered for political refugee
status on a laborious case-by-case basis. Many must flee

again when they cannot stay in the United States legally. Culture shock and the grief of losing family and home in Guatemala lead some people to simply become sick. And yet Maria was able to both document the articulation of the Guatemalan Mayan with this process better. Thank you, Maria, for the patience, fortitude and strength to do the work that led to this study. Thank you also for communicating it here with clarity and insight.

Professor Allan F. Burns
Department of Anthropology
University of Florida
Gainesville, Florida

CHAPTER ONE
INTRODUCTION

It is a historic tradition for the
American people to respond to refugee
problems. Our national celebration at
the rededication of the Statue of
Liberty reminded us of the spirit of
welcome which has inspired generations
of immigrants and refugees to seek new
lives in this country (Shultz, 1986).

Since 1982, Indiantown, Florida, has become a new home
base for an increasing number of Guatemalan refugees who
have fled their native homeland and are establishing a new
life in the migrant farmworker streams in the United States.
Health problems of migrants and of rural populations have
been well documented (Shenkin, 1974; Mustian, 1980) and
there is a growing body of literature on various health
related issues of refugee populations throughout the world,
including the United States. However, to date, little has
been documented of the special problems and issues of
meeting basic health care needs that face the Guatemalans as
refugees, migrants and undocumented aliens.

Increasing concern and expenditures for health care
throughout the world has underlined the need for a greater
understanding of people's attitudes and behaviors regarding
the state of their health and the forms of care that are
considered acceptable. This has direct implications for

1

considered acceptable.   This has direct implications for
policy formation and program development at all levels.
Effective community health planning warrants this kind of
understanding that social scientists can help provide.

    The goal of this study is to analyze the impact of
existing health care resources on the perceptions, beliefs,
knowledge and health-seeking behavior of selected Guatemalan
refugee families in Indiantown.   Specific health problems
will be identified, and recommendations for their solutions
will be based on these findings.   Therefore, in addition to
providing an ethnographic report on refugee adaptations to
life in the United States, this is an applied project aimed
at making the health and service community of Indiantown
better able to serve this and other populations.

THE EMERGING REFUGEE CRISIS

    While the study of change has had an important role in
anthropology over the years, it has become increasingly
clear that anthropologists and other social scientists can
no longer take a passive role in simply studying the
consequences of change.   It is evident that the application
of the skills and knowledge social scientists have gained
may help to ease the commonly disruptive effects of such
world-wide events as development and modernization,

urbanization, wars and natural disasters. Such events often result in the uprooting and displacement of groups of people and even whole communities, creating refugees.

The offical 1951 United Nations Convention, which was extended by the 1967 Protocol, defines a refugee as

> Any person who, owing to a well-founded fear of persecution for reasons of race, religion, nationality, membership of a particular social group or political opinion, is outside the country of his nationality and is unwilling to avail himself to the protection of that country; or who, not having a nationality and being outside the country of his former habitual residence as a result of such events, is unable or, owing to such fear, unwilling to return to it (UNHCR, 1979).

In subsequent General Assembly resolutions, the mandate of the U. N. High Commission on Refugees has been extended to include: displaced persons who are outside their country of former habitual residence, and are in a refugee-like situation; former refugees and displaced persons repatriated to their country or origin; and, in specific cases, persons displaced as a result of man-made disasters within their own country (Simmonds, et al., 1983: 2).

The need to define refugee and refugee status has been primarily motivated by the fact that the last three decades have been witness to an unprecedented rise in the number of refugee situations requiring international assistance. In order to allocate resources to refugee situations, aid-giving agencies find it imperative to provide such guidelines to determine when, where and what kind of assistence will be provided.

The numbers of refugees that are known are staggering. In 1951 there were about one and a quarter million officially recognized refugees in the world. In 1982 there were about ten million, of which at least half of whom were children. Unofficial estimates put the number closer to eighteen million. In 1979 large numbers of refugees and dsiplaced Somalians were in the headlines, as were the Indochinese "boat people." In 1980 some 300,000 Khmer people fled Kampuchea into Thailand and severe drought threatened much of East Africa (Simmonds, et al, 1983: 3-5). Famine has continued to displace many thousands of people in Ethiopia. By mid-1982 there were an estimated 2.5 million Afghan refugees in Pakistan (UNHCR, 1982). More recently, the political situations in Central America, South Africa and the Middle East continue to generate yet more refugees and displaced persons. One must not forget, however, that not included in these figures are the many hundreds of thousands of refugees that are not officially recognized by host governments and, perhaps most unfortunately, various aid-giving organizations. The Guatemalan refugees in the United States are among these.

By 1982, the first trickle of Guatemalan refugees reached Indiantown, a small migrant town in southern Florida. Fleeing a country devastated by increasing political violence and extreme poverty, these ancestors of the ancient Maya sought refuge in the land of El Norte, the land of promise, opportunity and peace (Ashabranner, 1986). Since 1980 thousands of Indian peasants fled their country to escape death squad activity and forced relocation to "model communities," part of a government strategic hamlet program. It is estimated that between 1980 and 1983 at least 4,500 Guatemalans died during their flight, and those who were able to cross the border into Mexico often found shelter in refugee camps that soon became overcrowded and plagued with various problems of camp life (Durand, 1984).

In January 1983 the number of Guatemalan refugees living in Mexico was estimated to be 32,800, according to figures from the Mexican Committee for Aid to Guatemalan Refugees and the Office of the United Nations High Commissioner in Mexico City. Approximately half of them arrived after the coup d'etat of March 23, 1982 (OAS, 1983). By 1984, the estimated number of refugees in Mexico was 42,000, not including some 60,000 "clandestine" refugees living in Mexico as undocumented aliens (Durand, 1984:9).

After an often long and dangerous trek, many Guatemalan refugees entered the United States as illegal aliens. Some went to major urban centers to find work, others joined the agricultural migrant streams. Chapter Two describes life for the Guatemalan population in Indiantown which, by the peak of the 1986 harvest season, had grown to nearly six hundred, including men, women and children.

PUBLIC HEALTH AND HEALTH BEHAVIOR

The number of Guatemalans who have made Indiantown their home-base is only a fraction of the estimated 8,000 Guatemalans living thoughout the United States. However, they constitute an increasing proportion of local Health Department and Health Center clients. Questions health workers in Indiantown have been asking include: how are their health needs to be assessed, and how can health workers help them to meet those needs? Also, how is the health of the Guatemalan population related to the health of the greater Indiantown community? Indeed, it is not unlikely that other communities along the migrant stream may be asking similar questions about their Guatemalan clientele or would-be clientele.

A growing concern for community development and public health issues during the 1940s and 1950s attracted social scientists to examine the behavior of people in the face of sickness and in the presence of medical and other resources

for health. Anthropologists in particular recognized the
need for projects to take cultural factors into
consideration when introducing change into a community
(Paul, 1955; 1963; Foster and Anderson, 1978). It is now
generally appreciated among medical personnel and health
planners that sensitivity to significant cultural and social
differences between groups is paramount for the successful
provision of health services (Jelliffe and Bennett, 1962;
Milio, 1967; Reynolds, 1976; PAHO, 1984).

Of concern to health care administrators is the ability
of existing programs to successfully address problems and
provide solutions that are both cost and time efficient.
Recognition of the human factor in health and illness,
however, also demands that efforts directed toward better
community health be flexible or "custom-built" (Hanlon and
Pickett, 1984). Such flexibility is generally difficult to
achieve in a rigidly structured health care system in which
policy development often does not included any real
contigency planning, and when continued funding for programs
depends on their ability to meet certain minimal standards
and goals that may be difficult to measure (USDHEW, 1977).

The most common evaluations used to determine program
progress are based on epidemiological studies of program
impact on nutritional and health status, and process
evaluations of the functioning of health programs, projects

and their personnel.   However, such studies are not
designed to address questions regarding the effect of
programs on actual health behavior.

It has been noted that in the developed countries many
of the changes that have occured in the prevalence of
diseases, particularly communicable diseases, have been the
result of measures that have involved little or no
individual participation, such as improved sanitation
systems, and mass immunizations (Winslow, 1980). Similarly,
Cipolla shows that the patterns of mortality in South
American nations since the 1930's have taken place primarily
among the diseases that do not require individual effort in
order to be amenable to public health measures.   "When
deaths due to causes that require modern medicine or
individual actions, such as personal hygiene, are
considered, it may be seen that these still constitute an
exceedingly high percentage of all deaths" (Cipolla, 1983:
64).

If the goal of public health is not only to provide
services for people but also to get people to accept an
increasing responsibility for their health, then questions
regarding factors that influence health behavior--what
people do in order to maintain or restore their health,
ranging from individual to collective behavior, and
why--must be addressed.   A sociocultural approach views

such behavior as part of a health culture, which includes
both cognitive and social systems, beliefs and practices
(Weidman, 1979). Health culture descriptions, thus, provide
a framework of rules and meanings for culturally appropriate
behavior.   It becomes possible, then, to describe how a
health program, as the manifestations of a particular health
culture, interacts with aspects of another health culture.
Such an approach can help to pin-point problem areas and
suggest a course for action that will be "custom-built" for
the community.

METHODOLOGY

To achieve the goal of this study, it was necessary to
1) describe the existing health and nutrition knowledge,
beliefs and practices of the selected households; 2) analyze
what factors affect people's perceptions of health care
programs and services; and 3) examine how and to what extent
the various health resources available to these people have
affected their understanding of health and illness and their
health-seeking behavior.

Murray L. Wax has described the nature of scientific
inquiry in the social sciences as in a dynamic conflict
between the search for precision and the search for accuracy
(1970:48-51). The relationship between these is viewed as a

dialectic in which the social scientist must strive to achieve these goals without the sacrifice of one for the other. If observation is primary to scientific inquiry, the what, who, when, where, why and how of the observations to be made must be determined to best explain and predict, accurately and precisely, the phenomenon to be studied. Not all observations may be planned in advance, however, and the social scientist must also be open to judge which of these observations made are relevant to the problem at hand.

In the study of behavior within a socio-cultural reality, the social scientist may utilize a series of complementary methodologies. For example, ethnographic insight may explain certain phenomena that sociological methods such as the sample survey may be able to measure precisely, but not accurately due to misunderstanding language or cultural events. Ethnography depends on observations and data gathering in a variety of social fields for accuracy. It also depends on the use of not one but many techniques and methods in order to maximize the number of observations.

A variety of techniques were employed to describe and explain the health behavior of Guatemalan refugees in Indiantown. Basic ethnographic methods where used for the recording of the sociocultural context of health-related beliefs, perceptions and behavior. This included formal and informal interviews and participant observation in Indiantown of everyday activities as will be discussed in detail in the following section on the field experience. Much of the groundwork and preparation for this actually began in December 1984, and during subsequent visits to Indiantown throughout 1985. In February, 1986 I moved to Indiantown to conduct more intensive and extensive field work. This last phase lasted three and a half months.

The core of this research consisted of a series of 63 in-depth interviews with members of selected families, primarily women. Much of the information presented on health beliefs and perceptions is based on what I learned from thirteen key informants and their families (here referring to the nuclear family). These are representative of the major groups that make up the Guatemalan community in Indiantown: the Catholics; Seventh Day Adventists and Evangelists; early arrivals to Indiantown; recent arrivals; young couples; and older families. Observations made of other families complemented these. All formal interviews were conducted in the family home. Informal interviews took place in a variety of settings, including during rides to and from the store, the Health Department in Stuart, and the like, when engaged in participant observation.

Much was learned from those who had already spent a great deal of time working with the Guatemalans, primarily the volunteers of the local Catholic service organization, the Holy Cross Service Center (El Centro), and the Indiantown health care workers. Health workers were only interviewed in the clinical setting formally and informally in the course of my acting as a Spanish translator for a client. Living in the Service Center's volunteer house with the volunteers afforded me ample opportunity to appreciate the difficult conditions, characteristic of small town life and low budget offices, under which the volunteers must work.

Since households with children five years old and younger are the focus of this study, a census was conducted of the Guatemalan population to assist in the selection of representative households. The census results include information on fifty-seven households, and 443 individuals. Census data included number of household members, identification of head of household, family relations, their age, sex, literacy, years of schooling, religion, occupation, length of time of residence in Indiantown, length of time in flight, place of origin, use of health care facilities previous to and since arrival to Indiantown (Appendix A).

In addition to the traditional ethnographic methods of interviews and participant observation and developing a sample survey for data collection, supplementary information

was provided by the Office of the County Commissioner and
the Division of Environmental Health in Stuart, primarily
related to epidemiological and other studies of Indiantown
conducted by these offices.

THE FIELD EXPERIENCE

Once it was realized that they were not Mexican, but
Guatemalan Indian refugees, and that the usual methods and
procedures were not very effective, the Indiantown
nutritionist contacted anthropologist Allan Burns of the
University of Florida, Department of Anthropology, asking
for some advice, as Burns has worked with Mayan people in
Mexico. In particular, the nutritionist was concerned
because many Guatemalan women had joined the Woman, Infant
and Child (WIC) program. Professor Burns told me about this
situation and I was intrigued. I had just moved to Florida
from Los Angeles where I had worked with other Central
Americans within the context of a community clinic for
refugees.

In December, 1984, I first went to Indiantown on a one
day "scouting" mission. I visited the Health Department and
briefly met with the nutritionist and public health nurses
working there. A preliminary problem was identified by the
nutritionist regarding the need to understand more about the

food habits of the Guatemalan WIC clients and their
families. It was agreed that a study of Guatemalan food
habits would be useful to the nutritionist to be better able
to target problem areas and possible approaches to their
solution. With this immediate goal in mind along with the
idea that this may develop into a thesis project, I began to
make regular trips to Indiantown, to assist as
Spanish/English translator during the busy WIC "Guatemalan
Wednesdays" and to conduct interviews, all within the
clinical setting. A report to the Health Department
documents the results of this preliminary study on the
refugees' food habits (Miralles, 1985).

While I had no knowledge of their Maya language,
Kanjobal, there were generally at least three or four other
Kanjobal women or an occasional man present who had enough
knowledge of Spanish to act as translator from Kanjobal to
Spanish. I could then translate from the Spanish to English
for the nurses, and then the process was reversed in the
course of dialogue. As such, conducting any interview
between health worker and client was often a laborious and
frustrating procedure.

It is generally acknowledged that there is really no
substitute for knowing the first language of a group of
people, and that despite some of the positive aspects of
having a translator, such as offering useful insights, the

negative aspects are heavy indeed, including inaccurate or incomplete translation, interviewee confidentiality, and interpreter bias. One positive aspect of using Spanish, the Guatemalans' second language, as the primary mode of communication, however, was that it was easier to ensure a more thorough interview by constant verification of what was being understood by the interviewer with what was actually being communicated by the interviewee. Despite this generally annoying process, however, the rewards came later as friendships began to develop outside of the context of the health department.

In February, 1986, I moved to Indiantown to conduct the field work on which this study is based. I had previously presented a proposal of my research intentions to the Holy Cross Service Center, a local Catholic organization working closely with the Guatemalan population in Indiantown in providing a myriad of services. Two other University of Florida anthropology graduate students had worked in Indiantown previous to this, and thus, the Service Center personnel were familiar with the anthropology program. The Service Center expressed interest in the proposed project and provided me with considerable support, including providing me with an occassional place to spend the night when needed, and with housing during the period between February and May, 1986.

I had set up several tasks to accomplish while in Indiantown. First, I felt that it was important that, due to the nature of my interest (health can be a very private and personal matter), that I not be identified as working for either one of the major community service groups involved with the welfare of the Guatemalan community—the local Catholic Church, the Health Department and Health Center—yet I hoped that the results of the study would be of interest and of use to all.

I had to create a multiple faceted role for myself that included being a translator for the Health Department, and volunteering in some of the tasks for the Church's Service Center, including providing transportation, and conducting the census of the Guatemalan community. The Service Center, which has provided the needy population in Indiantown with a wide gamut of social services and support for the past eight years, maintains a small but committed full-time permanent staff, including a Guatemalan who was professionally employed in Guatemala as a community developer. The staff is generally complemented by two or three volunteers working on a one-year contract.

However, this approach in which the social scientist is seen as a culture broker or a facilitator for information exchange assumes that one can learn all, know all, or be all to everyone in the community. By participating in many of the activities in both organizations, but not actually being a full "member" of either, I hoped to be able to gain a unique, if not more holistic perspective of how they functioned, their views, and how their actions where perceived and received by others. By the same token, however, mine was an ambiguous role and as such participation was necessarily limited. I also learned that this approach did not leave room for dealing with conflicts of interest within and between groups and factions of the health and service community.

The ambiguity that resulted from this approach was picked up by my informants, both among the Guatemalans and many of the health workers. I often found it necessary to explain repeatedly that I would be staying in Indiantown for only a few months, and that as a student I was trying to learn as much as I could about the people in Indiantown and their experiences. Some took this as an opportunity for the airing of grievances and asking that I take action on their behalf. Thus, my role included that of a facilitator and of advocacy.

This role also provided a medium for channeling tensions between the Indiantown Health Unit and the Health Department in Stuart. Fueled by my initial neglect to inform the County Health Department offices of my activities in Indiantown, to follow proper procedures in filing liability insurance forms and the like, I found myself in the middle of an impasse in a long-standing communication problem between Indiantown and Stuart health workers. The Indiantown Health Department workers, primarily the WIC nutritionist, had been requesting additional support from their superiors in Stuart since prior to my arrival in Indiantown. This included among others the hiring of more bilingual clerks, additional clerks in general, and greater consideration for those who had to commute to Indiantown.

Unfortunately, those working in Stuart were not familiar with the Indiantown clinical situation and thus were not sympathetic to the problems of the Indiantown personnel. For example, given the unusual difficulties presented by the Guatemalan WIC clients, WIC guidelines were not strictly followed in that nutrition classes were often necessarily omitted in favor of individual nutritional counseling. Also, in the absence of Health Department translators, outside translators, including myself and Service Center volunteers, volunteered to assist as needed, acting in good faith.

It can not be denied that these actions were contrary to current Health Department policy and stipulations, and thus, in March, 1986, the situation came to a head. The Director of Nursing and the Director of WIC came to Indiantown to see for themselves what was happening there.

In spite of the many unfortunate events that led up to this
confrontation, there is no doubt that the few ensuing visits
to the Indiantown Health Unit provided a positive learning
experience for all concerned, and the Health Department's
commitment to improving the delivery of health care services
to Kanjobal people in Indiantown is commended.

On any given day a visitor to Indiantown could have
found me engaged in any number of activities. I did not
restrict my actions to only the Guatemalans, but rather
hoped to gain a better understanding of the dynamics of the
larger community of Indiantown. This includes a richly
varied population of blacks, whites, Mexicans and
Mexican-Americans, Puerto Ricans, Catholics, Seventh Day
Adventists, Pentacostals, migrants and non-migrants, the
employed and unemployed, the old and the young.

Activities included going to the fields to pick
oranges, sitting in waiting rooms for hours in the Social
Security office, clinics and hospitals, supermarket lines,
and attending various church services two or three times a
week, or just sitting on someone's porch or doorstep for a
while and chatting. I joined other volunteers in teaching
English on Tuesday evenings in the Catholic elementary
school to classes that included all age groups, men and
women, Mexicans and Guatemalans. I also gave some private
lessons to some of my informants who, in exchange, taught me

much more than the few words in Kanjobal I managed to learn.
Going door to door to conduct the census also provided a way
to meet people.   Perhaps most importantly, my automobile
allowed me not only to provide a valuable service, but was
also a major key to the community as a whole.

In this chapter I have described the anthropological
and health issues of refugees and other migrants.   As an
interprofessional   research   project,   methodological
considerations and techniques used for data collection of
Guatemalan   health   behavior   in   Indiantown   are   both
qualitative and quantitative.   A description of Indiantown
is provided in Chapter Two, accompanied by an ethnographic
and historical account of the Guatemalans' flight from their
homeland to their adaptations to life in the United States.
Chapters Three and Four address the beliefs and perceptions
about health and illness and the health seeking behavior of
the Guatemalans in Indiantown.   Chapter Five summarizes
these   findings,   and   Chapter   Six   provides   some
recommendations as to how such knowledge may be incorporated
into   existing   programs,   including   health   and   nutrition
education, as well as overall community development, thereby
making them more relevant to the sociocultural reality of
the population at hand.

CHAPTER TWO
THE PLACE AND THE PEOPLE

This chapter sets the stage for the arrival of the Kanjobal Mayans from Guatemala to Indiantown. Indiantown is described in terms of location, the services and programs available that make this an attractive town for an agricultural migrant work force. An ethnographic background of the Guatemalan refugees is then provided followed by a description of some defining characteristics of this specific population in Indiantown today. Finally, the health status of Indiantown is compared to other Florida migrant towns, demonstrating that, in at least one major area of Indiantown, prevalence of certain communicable diseases and overall poor environmental health conditions are positively correlated with lower income levels and overcrowding.

THE PLACE: INDIANTOWN, FLORIDA

> In addition to all of these modern
> conveniences, strategic location and
> industrial advantages, Indiantown offers
> the spirit and legend of Osceola, the
> chief of the Seminoles, to the people who
> inhabit this "Community Planned For
> Pleasant Living"--a scenic, open-air
> setting where they can live and work with
> zest in an atmosphere of natural beauty
> (de Marcellus and Knowlton, n.d.).

This introduction to Indiantown, which appears in a
pamphlet available from the Indiantown Chamber of Commerce,
may seem somewhat ironic to many current Indiantown
residents. Founded at the turn of the century, it has
received many peoples from many places, expanding and
contracting each year with the ebb and flow of the seasonal
migrant stream. An unincorporated town, Indiantown is like
so many other small migrant towns throughout the nation,
sharing many of the same pros and cons of rural life.

From the City of Okeechobee, Indiantown lies some
thirty-five miles south on State Road 710 and thrity-three
miles north of West Palm Beach. Stuart, the seat of Martin
County, lies twenty miles to the north-east. The St. Lucie
Canal demarcates the town's southern extension. State Road
710, known as Warfield Boulevard in town, is bifurcated by a
single traffic signal and is the "main drag" through the
town. The two supermarkets, a bar, the new liquor store,
the Seminole Country Inn, the Indiantown News office, the
Martin County Courthouse Annex (which houses the Indiantown
Health Department Unit), the ice cream parlor, the hardware
store, an automotive supply store, the beauty salon, the
telephone company, the pharmacy, the department store, a
tire and service center, a fried chicken restaurant, several
filling stations and mini-markets all line Warfield
Boulevard. One block from the traffic light off of

Wardfield Boulevard is the Post Office, the laundromat, the Migrant Housing Office, the Holy Cross Service Center and thrift store (see Figure 2.1).

In 1980 Indiantown's population was 3,383. It represented an ethnic and racial potpourri which included Whites, Blacks, Mexicans, Mexican-Americans, Puerto Ricans, and was beginning to include a growing number of Haitian refugees. Industrial employment is available in the area through an electric steel mill, a plastics molding plant, a major aircraft research and development firm, citrus processing, and construction. However, the more than 50,000 acres of citrus groves, and several vegetable fields that surround Indiantown provide employment for the large migrant work force that makes this its home base. This East Coast migrant stream consists of two major routes, both of which begin in the counties surrounding and south of Lake Okeechobee. One route, followed mainly by blacks, extends north from that area to Beaufort, South Carolina; New Bern, North Carolina; the eastern shore of Maryland, and central New York. The second route, followed primarily by Mexicans and Mexican-Americans moves northward through Alabama to northeastern Ohio and Michigan (Shenkin, 1974:6).

Among the services available in Indiantown that make it an attractive place to live are four schools that together provide education up to the eigth grade level. High school

1 "El Centro" Holy Cross Service Center
2 U.S. Post Office
3 Yellow Camp
4 Warfield Elementary School
5 Holy Cross Church and Hope Rural School
6 White Camp
7 Blue Camp
8 New Hope Community
9 Courthouse Annex/Health Department Unit
10 Florida Community Health Center
11 Market
12 Market
13 Indiantown Middle School

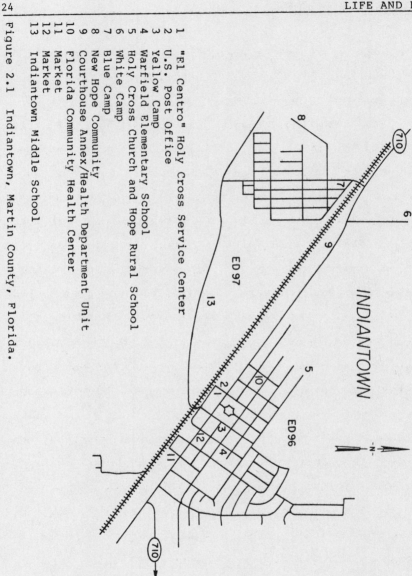

Figure 2.1 Indiantown, Martin County, Florida.

students are bused to a nearby facility. In addition, Migrant Education and Day Care, and adult education programs are available. Indiantown Non-Profit Housing offers its services for those in need, and the New Hope Community, started in 1982, provides housing for sixty migrant families, or 350 people.

The Seaboard Air Line Railroad parallels State Road 710, bringing passengers and freight through town at least twice a day. Together, these divide the town physically into two major areas, in the United States Census Bureau recognized as Enumeration Districts 96 and 97. Each Enumeration District (ED) is made up of small neighborhoods that blend into each other. Little Ranch Estates, Indianwood, Indiantown Park, and Oak Acres comprise ED 96. Booker Park, New Hope, Westbrook, Fernwood Forest and the Palm Oaks Estates comprise ED 97.

The majority of the Guatemalans in Indiantown live in three "camps," designated by the color of the paint on the buildings. Yellow Camp, once popularly known as the Roach Palace, is the oldest apartment complex in town available to migrant workers. These two-room apartments and neighoring bungalows total eighteen apartments in the middle of Indiantown Park. Guatemalans are also beginning to rent houses in the surrounding area. White Camp, a migrant housing unit located at the north-west end of town, has

eleven small single-family dwellings, but may house many
more families and single persons. This migrant housing is
owned and managed by a grower in the area, and residents
must be employed by this grower.

The largest of the camps is Blue Camp located in the
Booker Park area. Nearly two-thirds of the refugees live in
the Booker Park Area, and many of these live in this large
two-story apartment complex with seventy apartments. While
there are some single room apartments with no private
plumbing facilities, most have two rooms and a bathroom.
The front room doubles as a kitchen/dining area and bedroom.
Appliances generally include a hot plate for cooking and a
refrigerator. Other houses in the Booker Park area vary in
condition and size, from small single family units,
trailers, and houses sub-divided for two or more families.
Some have no electricity, and many have no heated water.
Indeed, this Booker Park Area of Indiantown has been of
concern to county public health workers for many years.

A community block survey conducted by the Environmental
Health Division of the Martin County Public Health Unit in
1984 reported the following:

> Booker Park ... has historically been
> known for its poor sanitation and its
> extreme contrast with the affluent
> coastal cities of Stuart and Hobe Sound.
> The large number of garbage sites,

overflowing septic tanks, farm animals,
privies, mosquitos and flies make this
an area of primary concern in the spread
of communicable disease (Washam and
Sims, 1985).

The results of the sanitary survey revealed that
approximately 90% of wastewater systems consisted of
cesspools, and at least 50% of waste water tanks had raw
sewage overflowing to ground surfaces and drainage ditches.

The depressed nature of the area is readily noticeable
to the casual observer of the Booker Park area (see Table
2.1). In addition, the epidemiological survey identified a
higher than average rate of communicable diseases in
Indiantown as compared to the rest of Martin County, with
many of the diseases originating in the Booker Park Area
(see Appendix B). In 1986, the sanitation survey was
repeated and some improvements had been noted. However, the
overall problems persist. In February, 1986, a $650,000
federal grant was awarded to improve sanitation facilities
but due to lack of community support and participation as
well as other logistic difficulties, progress has been
minimal.

INTER-ETHNIC RELATIONS

As the most recent in a series of minority groups to
come to Indiantown, the Guatemalans are at the bottom of the

Table 2.1   Comparison of Household and Family Income   for
              ED96 and ED97, 1979.

	ED96	ED97	ED96 =100	ED97
Median Age	24.1	21.4		
Population	1,895	1,488	100	78
No. families	444	295	100	66
No. households	507	436	100	86
Median household income	$21,155	$8,810	100	41
Median family income	$21,645	$10,074	100	46
Aggregate family income	$11,646,040	$3,913,445	100	33
No. persons above poverty level	1,747	796		
No. persons below poverty level	121	521		

Source: 1980 United States Census, Tables 2, 3, 69, 70,
           74, and 91 for Indiantown, Florida.

social totem pole in many ways. The first few families to
come to Indiantown did not represent a threat to the
residents of the town, their small stature and low profile
made them almost invisible. However, since their numbers
have climbed dramatically over a short period of time
several problems have arisen, especially with regard to
inter-ethnic relations. Many of these emerging tensions
spring from increased competition for scarce, indeed
limited, housing, and employment opportunities. This
situation also leaves much room for abuse and exploitation
by landlords, other tenants, and employers.

Some of the older residents of Indiantown feel that
there are too many Guatemalans living there. One forty-year
black resident living in Booker Park stated that, "a couple
of families here and there are alright . . . they don't
cause no problem, no complaint there, but when they all
come here and get drunk all the time . . . they ruin the
place with their garbage. They're too many."

While most Indiantown residents who attend the local
Catholic church are aware of the situation leading up to the
refugees flight from Guatemala, many other Indiantown
residents are not, much less do they know where Guatemala
is. Their distinctive language and style of dress set them
apart from other more familiar groups.

The Guatemalans have received much press and attention
from the service community, primarily the Service Center,
and from journalists interested in the the refugees' story.
This has resulted in a perceived, if not actual, redirection
of Service Center energies and resources toward the
Kanjobales. Some of the other clients of the Service Center
perceive that these efforts are at the expense of other
needy groups.   Unfortunately, the Service Center, as a
primary and highly visible helping-organization within the
community, is particularly vulnerable to such criticism.

Signs of resentment may be evidenced from Mexicans and
Mexican-Americans who fail to understand what is so special

about "los indios" ("the Indians"), a term which is generally considered to be derrogatory. Among the Mexican-American children, the Guatemalans are referred to as "watermelons", and their language and customs are very strange to them.

Some of the black youths take advantage of the Guatemalans' small stature and less aggressive nature compared to many Mexicans, and easily overtake them, knowing that many of the men carry all of their money on them because they have no bank accounts. The Guatemalans refer to the blacks, American, Haitian and Jamaican alike, as "moyos" and are for the most part wary of them.

White people are called "bolis", the name of a small round white bread sold in Guatemala and Mexico. Although relations between the Guatemalans and whites tend to be very limited, some white youths in particular have also expressed their sympathy with these "Spanish people" by slashing automobile tires and other such vandalism. As one might expect, the Guatemalans do not understand why these things happen to them. They state that they keep to themselves and do not know why people they do not even know would want to damage their possessions. In addition, some medical personnel have been accused by volunteer workers of treating their Guatemalan patients unkindly, suggesting, for example, that the women should want to be sterilized because, like animals, they have so many children (Davey, 1986). Others perceive the Kanjobal as a hard-working people who are irresponsible when it comes to drinking and driving, not a totally unfounded observation.

MAYANS IN INDIANTOWN

The homeland of the Guatemalan refugees is in the Northwest Cuchumatan highlands of Guatemala, within the Department of Huehuetenango. More specifically, the majority are from the municipio of San Miguel Acatan and surrounding aldeas or hamlets, including Sundelaj, Ixlahuitz, Yalaj, Chimban, Ixcanaj and others. There are also some from the towns of San Raphael de la Independencia and San Marcos, and the larger towns of Cuilco and Barrillas.

The population in this area is characterized by a high proportion of Indians of Mayan descent (Early, 1982). Although most of the refugee men and a handful of the women have a good speaking command of Spanish, the native language is Kanjobal, one of the twenty-four Mayan languages spoken in Guatemala. There is a smaller non-Kanjobal speaking group in Indiantown comprised of people from the predominantly ladino town of Cuilco. In 1959, it was estimated that the total number of Kanjobal speakers was

near 42,000 (Flores:23).   In 1973 figures estimated the
population to be approximately 80,000 (Davis, 1973:3).   More
recently, however, due to massive migration and heavy death
squad activity, reliable estimates are not available.

Traditionally, the economy of this region in Guatemala
has been based primarily on subsistence agriculture and some
small scale industry (Wagley 1967:60-66).   For more than
twenty years, however, due in great part to the increasing
problem of land shortage for cultivation throughout the
region (Castillo, 1986:69), the San Miguel area has been
characterized by regular migrant labor movements to various
plantation zones throughout the country.   Most of the
refugees in Indiantown were farmers, some with their own
land, some working part-time on large farms and coffee and
banana plantations.   Insufficient land, low productivity
levels on available lands, and lack of funds with which to
buy fertilizer have forced many throughout the highland
region to seek supplemental employment elsewhere (Applebaum,
1967).

During the peak of the 1986 citrus harvest there were
an estimated 600 Guatemalan men, women and children in
Indiantown.   Many came directly to Indiantown after crossing
the Mexican-United States borders, while others made their
way to Florida after spending a season or two elsewhere,
including   California, Washington, Arizona, Texas, and

Virginia. That most of the refugees are from San Miguel is primarily a result of a network of relatives and friends that characterizes a great proportion of Guatemalan families in Indiantown. The complete extent to which families and single persons are related has not been determined at this point, but it is suggested that the majority of families and single persons have at least one brother, brother-in-law, sister, or cousin also living in town. Often, whole families or groups travelled together believing that a family member or good friend already living in Florida could help them to find a place to live and a job.

Housing is often a cramped and crowded situation, with two, sometimes three families sharing a single apartment or house. Sometimes, a family will sub-rent space out to single men or women needing a space. At one point, one house with two bedrooms and a single "common" room was occupied by fourteen unrelated single men who arrived in Indiantown together from Arizona. As a result of this housing crunch, there is a high mobility within Indiantown as people move about in search of more adequate living spaces. It is not unusual for the residents of the same apartment not to know each other's name, nor where they work. This often makes it difficult to keep track of people over time, or even over night.

Based on a census of 443 Guatemalans in Indiantown, 353 of whom knew their age, the average age is 18.8, with only twenty-two persons over 40 years old. This relatively young population is composed primarily of children and single men. The average number of children per family is 2.91, with most families having at least one child five years old and younger (Table 2.2 ; Figure 2.2).

Table 2.2   Sex by Age Distribution of Guatemalan Population
             in Indiantown, Florida (April, 1986).

Age (yrs.)	Total	Male	Female
0 - 5	78	35	43
6 - 10	36	15	21
11 - 15	25	10	15
16 - 20	59	31	28
21 - 25	50	30	20
26 - 30	40	27	13
31 - 35	25	22	3
36 - 40	18	11	7
41 - 45	11	7	4
46 - 50	7	5	2
51 - 55	2	1	1
56 - 60	2	2	0
Total	353	196	157

Mean Age: 18.8 years

Sex Distribution (n=430): Male: 262 (60%)
                           Female: 168 (39%)

Number of Families with children 0 - 5 yrs: 42
Single persons 16 years or older: 102 (81 M; 20 F)
Married persons 16 years or older: 112 (55 M; 57 F)

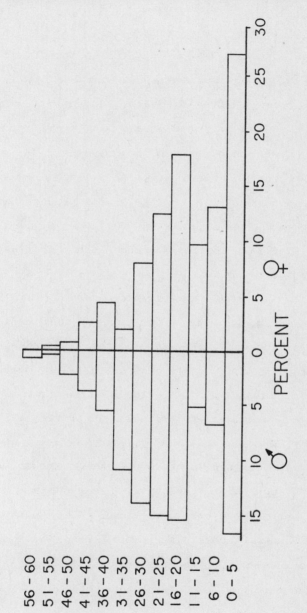

AGE (YRS.)

56 - 60
51 - 55
46 - 50
41 - 45
36 - 40
31 - 35
26 - 30
21 - 25
16 - 20
11 - 15
6 - 10
0 - 5

PERCENT

Figure 2.2   Sex by Age of Guatemalan Refugees, Indiantown, Florida
             (April, 1986)

Although most have not had any formal schooling, all of the men understand and speak Spanish somewhat, and some can read. Even fewer women have ever attended any school and the number of those who understand and speak Spanish is considerably lower than the men. The majority of children over five years old, however, are enrolled in school, and many are becoming fluent in English. Some parents have also been able to place their pre-schoolers in a day care center for migrant families, freeing working parents from having to find and pay for child care.

In nearly all families in which there are no infants less than three months old, both parents seek employment. There are two kinds of employment: contract and non-contract work. Contract work is highly desired, providng security of employment, at least for the period of time covered by the contract. Non-contract work is based on a variable hourly or piece-rate basis and is not guaranteed from one day to the next. These types of employment, known as "por contrato" and "por hora" respectively, characterize both the citrus and vegetable crops as well as nursey work. As a result, individual income when people find work may vary anywhere between sixty to two-hundred dollars a week, depending on the kind of employment, one's luck and the progress of the harvests.

Although individual and family incomes may vary considerably from week to week, certain expenses remain constant. These include the rent and food. Depending on how many roommates one has and the condition of the house, the rent may be as low as five dollars a week per individual to forty-five dollars a week per family for a single room apartment with no personal use plumbing. While some migrant housing requires each individual resident to pay a fixed amount, others kinds of housing have a fixed rent that may be divided by the number of people living there, thereby encouraging an overcrowed situation. This is all apart from any additional water and electricity expenses. The weekly food bill for single persons is between fifteen to twenty-five dollars. A family of five may spend between sixty-five and eighty dollars on food. Other common expenses persons may incur include child care (about five dollars a day per child), laundry, clothing, transportation, and medical expenses.

In the event that both husband and wife work, the woman retains control over the income she brings in and is responsible for decisions regarding its use. If only the husband brings in an income, he may allocate an amount to his wife from which she is expected to cover certain expenses. The responsibility for doing the food shopping may be either the man's or the woman's, often both sharing it. The degree of the woman's autonomy in decision making in general may depend on the context in which a decision needs to be made. For example, it may rely on her ability to speak Spanish or simply whether or not her husband is present at the time that a decision needs to be made.

Among the many things that the Guatemalans have had to learn in Indiantown include using the post office to send and receive correspondence, how use the washing and drying machines in the laundromat, how to buy hot food in the market, learn about certain products in the stores such as insecticides and how to use them, and how to enroll the children in school. Much guidance and assistance was offered by the Catholic priests and nuns and other Service Center volunteers.

Although the Kanjobal Guatemalans are unusual, they are only the latest in a steady immigration to Indiantown and credit must be given to the people in the markets, in the laundromats and throughout the town who have served as patient guides on inumerous occassions. One can only imagine the many number of times the cashiers at a local market have tried to explain, often in English, to a Guatemalan woman that she had picked out a cereal not covered by the WIC program, replaced it with the acceptable cereal, and then waited patiently as the mother signed the check with her "X."

The Guatemalans in Indiantown are by no means a homgenous group. Their experiences, while similar in many ways, also differ and this affects the relationships between them. A major division between people is religion. There are at least three religious denominations being practiced by the Guatemalans. There are about thirty-two Catholic families, most of which attend services in town with some regularity. Seventh Day Adventists, with twenty-four families, van-pool to services in West Palm Beach on Saturdays and some hold a Bible study group once a week at someone's home. A smaller group, made up of primarily single men are the Evangelists who attend a church in Indiatown.

Thirty-three families state that they do not practice any religion in particular. This does not imply a vacuum of spiritual convictions, but rather may be interpreted in various ways of which fear of responding is one. This may be due to the recent persecution in Guatemala of catequistas, the followers of the Catholic Action movement. Followers of this movement are concerned with purifying the practice of the Catholic religion in indigenous areas by removing all "pagan" elements, such as those associated with the native rituals of costumbres. The disruptive effects on community life as a result of the conflicts between the traditional Catholicism and the new orthodoxy have been noted in Momostenango (Tedlock, 1982:40-44). However, because of their efforts at community development in the areas of health care, provision of fertilizers, and the like, however, this group was viewed by the Guatemalan government as politically threatening. For this reason, it may be that persons in the census sample denied any relgious proclivity out of insecurity or fear.

Religiosity was not specifically addressed in this evaluation. It is clear, however, that some basic issues divide the these groups. Among these issues is that of heavy drinking, denounced by the Adventists and Evangelists who attribute much of the violence, "shameless behavior" and irresponsible spending of hard-earned money on beer. Another, not totally unrelated issues is that of prostitution and abandonment, again levied against the non-Adventists and non-Evangelists.

There is little doubt that prostitution and a high rate of alcohol and drug abuse are community-wide phenomena. There is some concern among the older Guatemalan population that some of the single men are frequenting local prostitutes and may be experimenting with illegal drug use. Many Kanjobal men arrange for Guatemalan women to come to Indiantown as companions after they have found a job. As a result of this and the more recent tide of younger unattached refugees, a few cases of abandonment have

occurred. The husband (common-law marriages among the
Kanjobal in Indiantown are the norm) may set up a separate
household, sometimes in another town, with the other woman.
Although the incidence of abandonment is, up to this point,
very low and is no doubt the exception, it is, nonetheless,
considered a very real threat, both to the very young
pregnant Kanjobal woman who may have entered into a
relationship somewhat unwittingly and to the woman who has
borne her mate several children.

There are also political rifts between the
Guatemalans. First, there is an element of resentment among
the early arrivals to Indiantown toward the more recent
arrivals. Those who left their country before 1985 feel
that the new arrivals, mostly single men, have come only
looking for work and to send dollars home. The first
arrivals submit that they had no choice but to leave
Guatemala because their lives were directly threatened.
Indeed, some of these problems are currently becoming
manifest as cases for political asylum are being brought to
court. Even among these first arrivals, there is tension
and distrust. This is a result of differing experiences
with the various political and military groups in Guatemala.
Some of the refugees, for example, fled the violence and
destruction by the army, while others tell tales of guerilla
abuses.

Life for the people in Indiantown revolves around making a living. The day begins at dawn as non-contract workers go to the pick-up points in town where they may find work. Others may be picked up by crew leaders with transportation, and some may go in their own car. For the Guatemalans, the morning and noon meals may be brought from home, usually consisting of some fresh warmed over tortillas, soup in a thermos, or other food in a container. At least one large thermos with water, or several cold cans of soda are also packed. Sometimes, a warm lunch may be bought at the market before going to work to be eaten throughout the day. Then, depending on the harvest schedule, work may end in the late afternoon or early evening. Usually, the end of the work day is signified by a visit to the market to buy some soda, a snack, or some item needed in the house.

As with other migrant workers, there are some groups among the Guatemalans that prefer to work together. Often they may be related, or they may simply work well together. For examle, the Adventists tend to all work together in the same crews. Wives generally work with their husbands, but women are more likely to have non-contract work.

Women may also bring in some money by baby-sitting, charging five dollars a day per child, or doing laundry by hand. There are also a few women who will cook for single

men, and in exchange will get a free meal. This occurs most
often when single men live with a family or couple, and the
woman will determine a weekly food budget, collect the bill,
do the shopping and cook for all.

     When not working in the fields, and especially on
festive occassions, many Guatemalans may be seen wearing
their traditional clothing. Many women will wear their
traditional handwoven huipil and corte and carry their loads
in woven blankets. They may wear many strands of
multi-colored necklaces and sparkeling earrings. The men
prefer the Mexican style ranch hats, and recently the most
popular ones have plumage in the front. Otherwise, every
man owns a baseball cap, and every woman owns at least one
bandana. Blue jeans and colorful sneakers are also popular
for everyone. Indeed, many Guatemalan teen-agers could
easily grace the covers of teen fashion magazines.

     Social life among the Guatemalans in Indiantown
revolves primarily around the family, the church, and
recreation as well as work. The immediate and extended
family are the prime units of social interaction. Since
households with many families may not be very intimate, men
and boys with bicycles and those few families with
automobiles criss-cross the town with great frequency,
especially on the weekends. However, because there is no
public transportation in town, and distances can be quite

large, visiting may be limited and many weeks may pass
before one sister or cousin sees another.   In the Booker
Park area in particular, many Guatemalans do not feel safe
to go about alone.

People generally become very familiar with the other
residents of the camp, be it Blue Camp or Yellow Camp.
Given the overcrowded living situation in these camps it is
not hard to meet people. Most people in the camps are quick
to recognize a stranger and are usually suspicious of
possible thieves. It is important to realize, however, that
in a place where your front door is your only door, rooms
are overcrowded, and where walls are thin, privacy is at a
premium, and the tensions between neighbors may run very
high.   In addition, news and rumors run faster than
lightening under these conditions. Small children play no
small role in this, as they may either be the instigators,
the spies sent by parents, or innocent by-standers that are
easily overlooked.

Church activities provide another major focus for
social interaction. The Catholic church offers a Spanish
mass once during the week in the evening, Saturday evening
and Sunday in which a Mayan catachist recites the gospel in
Kanjobal. A school bus is available to shuttle people to
and from the church on these days and is usually quite full.
The church also runs a small elementary school that is well

attended by several Guatemalan children, not all of whom may
be Catholic. A Guatemalan Youth Group, whose activities
include bible study and community service, is also sponsored
by the church.

The Adventists attend Spanish services on Saturday
mornings in West Palm Beach by means of a well-organized van
pool. There are several other Guatemalan families living in
West Palm Beach that also attend the same church, and many
are related to the people in Indiantown. The Guatemalans
generally occupy the same section of pews in the church,
somewhat apart from the rest of the Spanish-speaking
congregation, with the leader and his family to the head of
the group. A vital part of the services is the review of a
lesson from the bible. During the week, the adults meet in
a house to discuss this lesson in Kanjobal. The discussion
is led by a man considered to be a leader of the group, and
who is so recognized by the Adventist Church.

During part of the service all Kanjobal children, along
with the other children from the congregation, are separated
from their parents and taken to classrooms behind the church
where they are similarly taught a particular lesson from the
bible in Spanish. There may be a small presentation or
performance by all the children later in the service based
on this lesson. The Guatemalan parents as well as the
children enjoy this very much and may chide one another

afterwards on how a certain child sings or speaks. Upon
arrival in Indiantown after the services, it is time for
lunch, for visiting, or just relaxing. Some people may also
opt to spend the day in West Palm Beach to visit or to go to
a large flea market to buy a few things or socialize.

Recreation in Indiantown is somewhat limited. For many
people, a weekend is time to do the shopping, fixing the
car, cleaning the house, or simply relaxing. Some men have
formed a soccer club that meets occassionally to practice,
and others practice playing old and new songs on a marimba
that was carefully brought from Guatemala. Weekends are
also the most violent times in Indiantown in general, when
more fights accidents and deaths occur. This is also when
many Guatemalan men indulge in heavy beer drinking, an
increasing visible problem.

HEALTH CARE RESOURCES IN INDIANTOWN

There are several health care resources available to
the general population of Indiantown. In town the major
facilities include a county health unit which shares a
single story building with the sheriff's office and county
courthouse annex on the north-west edge of town, and a
community health center.

The Health Department unit is staffed by a full time
public health nurse and clerk, and provides basic public
health services such as immunizations and school health. It
also houses clinics that take place on specific days of the
week. These include family planning once a week (fee of ten
dollars), WIC three times a week, and more recently the
Improved Pregnancy Outcome (IPO) and Well-Baby programs once
a week. All services are offered between 8:00 A.M. and 4:30
P.M., Mondays through Fridays. Medications are not
available, and those clients requiring prescriptions are
referred to the community clinic. Among the Guatemalans,
this unit is known as "el Corte," because of its location in
the courthouse annex, and most of the programs are well
attended by the refugees. Indeed, two days a month are
necessarily set aside for "Guatemalan Wednesdays" and, while
primarily intended for the WIC program activities, it also
gives an opportunity to give vaccinations and make
appointments for other purposes.

"La clinica" is a community clinic located down the
road from the courthouse, closer to the center of town. The
Florida Community Health Center, Inc., a public corporation
with several branches throughout southeast Florida, is
geared to meeting the primary health needs of indigents and
migrant workers. Fees are determined on a sliding
ability-to-pay scale basis, requiring a minimum five dollar

payment for most services. Services provided at the clinic include: comprehensive screening, acute episode care, chronic disease management, basic in-house and major lab services, specialty and sub-specialty medical consultation, dental diagnostic and treatment, transportation, and X-ray services. The only services offered in both the Health Department and the clinica immunizations and family planning.

At the time of this investigation the staff included doctors and nurses who have several years of experience in the community, ranging from a minimum of three years to twelve. Currently there is no midwife on duty, although there was one previously, and the necessary facilities exist. The operating hours, Mondays, Wednesdays and Fridays from 9:00 A.M. to 5:30 P.M., and Tuesdays and Thursdays from 12:00 P.M. to 8:30 P.M., allow for working patients to come in after hours. The staff acknowledges that the Guatemalans are their best patients, sometimes coming early for an appointment.

Another major health resource facility available to the general population is Martin Memorial, a private hospital located in Stuart, the county seat, a little more than twenty-five miles east of Indiantown. Hospital services most utilized by Indiantowners are for medical emergencies, generally related to accidents, and birthing and related

delivery needs. In general, indigent fees are picked up by
the county. Indiantown clients may be referred to the
hospital for special diagnostic exams not available locally,
or for surgical needs. From there, they may be referred to
any of a number of specialists located in the hospital
vicinity for follow-up. Many Guatemalans have delivered
their babies in the hospital, and others have gone for
complaints ranging from unusual vaginal bleeding, severe
anemia, severe headaches, and minor surgery, primarily as a
result of automobile accidents.

Before the IPO program was moved to Indiantown in May,
1986, clients had to go to the Health Department in Stuart
for their pre-natal check-ups. Transportation to and from
various pick-up points in Indiantown and Stuart Health
Department is available three times a week through a shuttle
bus service, sponsored by the Mr. Siegel Council on Aging.
There is usually a minimal fee asked for these services. If
the schedule is not convenient, clients must arrange for
their own ride, perhaps with a Service Center volunteer, or
a friend with a car. Indeed, there is no doubt that
attendance is drastically affected by the availability of
alternate forms of transportation, primarily the volunteers
who also act as badly needed translators. Birth
certificates are also obtained from "Estuart," the name the

Guatemalans use to signify either the Health Department, or any one of the major super markets in Stuart.

There is one private physician who offers services in Indiantown. Offering family medicine and general practice services, this office is not open on a full time basis as the physician also works and lives in Palm Beach Gardens. As of the time of this study, no Guatemalans have utilized his services. Several physicians, medical clinics and a hospital are also located in the City of Okeechobee, located some thirty-five miles north of Indiantown, Fort Pierce, and in Palm Beach County to the south, all at least a three-quarter hour, if not more, drive from Indiantown. Persons may be referred to physicians in these areas by the Health Center if needed.

The Holy Cross Service Center has also been providing, somewhat sporadically, bimonthly Pregnant Women's meeting in the evenings. These meeting were organized by one of the female volunteers and a male Guatemalan community organizer working for the Service Center during the period from June, 1985 to August, 1986. They were targeted at educating pregnant women, usually numbering nine to fifteen at any one time, raising issues such as breast feeding versus bottle feeding and maternal nutrition. However, the meetings, held in the church school, depended heavily on the efforts of this volunteer to recruit women, provide transportation and organize session topics.   Meetings often were necessarily postponed, and once this volunteer was no longer available, all activity stopped but for a short while when another volunteer started similar activities, and then also left the Service Center.

GUATEMALAN HEALTH CARE RESOURCES IN INDIANTOWN

Many of the health care resources people relied on for their health needs in Guatemala do not exist in Indiantown. Among these, the Guatemalans note most frequently the conspicuous absence of farmacias and herb vendors where, in Guatemala, one could obtain any number of remedies, not available or recognised in Indiantown, that could be prescribed by the pharmacist himself without a physician's prescription.   One could also receive injections at the farmacia, a service the Guatemalans consider very useful and beneficial.   Also absent in Indiantown is any particular individual or individuals recognized as having special healing skills, known as a curanderos, or traditional curers.

There are, however, at least two Kanjobal midwives who have been available to give advice and treatment to women who seek it.   Both have also volunteered to be present at the Pregnant Women's meetings.   Both women had been

apprenticed to traditional midwives in Guatemala since they
were very young, one for more than ten years, the other for
about five years. Their vocations were also decided in
different ways: the first followed her mother's example, and
the second states that she was divinely inspired to pursue
midwifery. Their personalities and stlyes are very
different, and as a result, some women will seek help from
one or the other as a matter of personal choice. No one
interviewed questioned the capabilities either one.

     There are also at least three men trained by Catholic
missionaries in Guatemala to be promotores de salud, a
village level worker knowledgeable in first aid and
preventive medicine. One of these men was the coordinator
of the health promotor program in the San Miguel area.
Although he is reluctant to administer injections or provide
medications as he was expected to do in Guatemala, he is
still occassionaly sought out for advice.

MIGRANT AND RURAL HEALTH CARE IN FLORIDA

     The comparison has been made of rural health care
issues in the United States with health care in much of the
Third World. Common demographic characteristics include a
sparse population, low income levels, depressed educational
opportunities, poor infrastructural and environmental

factors (Klein, 1976; Mustian, 1980; Reynolds, et.al., 1976). Both areas demonstrate similar problems related to health status and health care delivery, including a lower proportion of physicians to rural populations compared to urban areas, the difficulty in obtaining and maintaining sufficient manpower, fewer facilities available, less accessibility (primarily in terms of financial and time constraints) of facilities, and low utilization rates of existing facilities. In both areas effective health care delivery must emphasize community health and prevention.

Under the rubric of rural health care is migrant health. Migrant health, however, in addition to those conditions mentioned above, presents other factors that often meant that many federal, state and county medical programs for indigents have failed to address the migrant. Some of these include residency requirements that a highly mobile group cannot meet, and proof of income levels for a spurious and non-continual employment status. Although migrants are probably worse off among the rural poor, it seems clear that the migrant health problem is not an isolated one, but is only one sector of the rural poor health problem. The general health status of migrants has been summarized as follows:

> Migrants ... seem to be much more ill,
> both chronically and acutely, than the
> large majority of Americans. Their

> specific pattern of diseases is not
> known, but they are probably subject to
> the same range of chronic illnesses as
> the majority of Americans, and, in
> addition, have superimposed on them the
> range of illnesses, both chronic and
> acute, that afflicted most Americans
> years ago (e.g., infectious diseases),
> plus occupational diseases.
> Unscientifically, many observers think
> that the hard work and deprivation that
> are the migrants' lot from early
> childhood make them old more quickly
> (Shenkin, 1974:12)

Like many refugee situations, often the development of
programs designed for agricultural migrant workers has been
both motivated and hampered by international and local
political concerns. These concerns where not only related
to labor conditions and labor supply, but also by concerns
on the part of federal, state and local health systems as to
the nature of a separate migrant health program and its
relation to existing public agencies and private services
(Shenkin, 1974:21-43).

A contributing factor complicating the issues of
migrant health care is that of the illegal migrant worker.
Guatemalan refugees in the United States are recognized by
the Federal government as illegal aliens and, as such, are
not elligible for various health services and assistance
offered other refugees. As illegal aliens they are also
excluded from assistance programs for indigents and other
deprived groups that are citizens. In attempting to meet

their health needs, therefore, Guatemalans in Florida
working as migrant agricultural workers must deal not only
those problems that might be expected of a refugee or
immigrant population in a new environment, but also the
fears of deportation which may discourage use of health
facilities which are available to them, and comprehending
the existing rural and migrant health care systems and
services offered.

Among the various investigations that preceded the
establishment of the federal Migrant Health Program in 1962,
was the classic study They Follow the Sun (Koos, 1957) that
attempted to determine the most pressing problems Florida
migrants face and how these problems are confronted and
solved. A few years later the results of a five year
interdisciplinary study (Browning and Northcutt, 1961)
brought to the public the plight of black migrant workers in
nearby Belle Glade, Palm Beach County, Florida. This study
was the first of its kind and was designed to plan, apply
and evaluate public health services to meet the needs of
migrant workers, particularly mothers and children. Part of
this same research, another study (Delgado, et al., 1961)
focussed on the eating patterns among the migrant families,
and, following Browning's recommendations for improved
nutrition education, was aimed at developing public health

techniques more adaptable to the migrants' cultural food
patterns .

Twelve years later, Families of the Fields (Kaufman,
1973) provided a complementary follow-up on the health
status of the Palm Beach County migrant families, also
focussing on nutritional concerns. Results compared with
the Ten State Nutrition Survey for low income groups, and
while there was an absence of nutritional deficiencies as
detected by medical examinations, biochemical data did
indicate a high prevalence of iron deficiency anemia and
dental problems related primarily to inadequate nutritional
intake and aggravated by intestinal parasites. In addition,
the impact of the existing nutrition education program (the
result of the Browning and Delgado studies) is evaluated for
observed changes in food habits and through follow-up
clinical examinations. Recommendations included the need
for early and continuing nutrition education consistency
with general health education programs in the schools and
community.

Although these studies were conducted over a decade
ago, much the same could be said for Indiantown today. What
these and studies elsewhere all would seem to indicate is
that the problems of migrant farm workers are not a health
problem; not a labor problem; not a welfare problem, nor an
agricultural problem, but rather are part of larger social

problems that plague many communities throughout the nation
(Browning and Northcutt, 1961:65).   It is within this
context that health care for the Guatemalan refugee
population must be considered.

Indiantown has been the home-base for peoples of
diverse backgrounds for many years. It has grown accustomed
to the constant ebb and flow of migrant workers that "follow
the sun" such that business is expected to slow down during
the off-season, and expected to boom again with the harvests
when the streets come alive and the single traffic light is
most appreciated. And when yet another group of people came
to live in Indiantown, it was relatively easy for the small
town to incorporate them into the normal course of events.
It is evident that this unique group of Mayan refugees has
been able to adapt to life in a new cultural and physical
environment.

CHAPTER THREE
HEALTH BELIEFS AND PERCEPTIONS

No human group lacks an explanation of
the conditions that must be fulfilled or
maintained for the individual to enjoy
good health, and no human group lacks
explanations of the causes of illness
(Clark, 1959:1)

This chapter will explore the some of the beliefs and
perceptions held by the Guatemalan refugees in Indiantown
regarding the current state of their health. This includes
a list of illnesses perceived to be most prevalent, their
causes and prescribed treatment. These are juxtaposed with
ethnographic accounts and epidemiological findings from
Guatemala to provide a basis for comparison of results.

Cognitive patterns of health and illness are central to
any health culture. Beliefs about the symptoms and causes
of illness, and the appropriate treatment are profoundly
interrelated. As Clark notes, "since curing practices are a
function of the beliefs on the nature of health and the
causes of illness, most curative procedures are
understandable and "logical" in light of those beliefs"
(1959:1). An inquiry into factors that influence health
seeking behavior, however, ust not only include beliefs but

58

also perceptions. For example, a mother may believe that breast-feeding is good, but that the milk goes bad when the mother works. If she works she may perceive that she does not have enough milk, and that the quality is poor. Her behavior may reflect these by both bottle-feeding and breast-feeding, or not breast-feeding at all. The difference between these terms are subtle but noteworthy.

Perceptions and beliefs about illnesses most problematic in Indiantown, their causes and appropriate cures were asked of thirteen refugee families with children five years old and younger and with both parents present and repsonding to the quesitonnaire. A total of eleven problems were reported, seven of them with greater frequency (Table 3.1). This is by no means a complete inventory of disease and illness, nor of health-related beliefs, but rather reflects the major concerns of refugee families in Indiantown.

ILLNESSES CAUSED BY AN HUMORAL IMBALANCE

Among the most well documented theories of health and illness in Mesoamerica is that of the humoral dichotemy of hot and cold. Imported to the New World by way of the Spanish, the wet and dry component of the old hippocratic quadratic disappeared in time, apparently along with many of

Table 3.1   Illnesses Perceived to be Most Problematic in Indiantown, their Causes and Cures

Illness	Cause	Cure
Diarrhea (13)	weather (12)	protect body and give liquids (10)
	bad water (13)	protect body and give liquids (13)
	fever (10)	protect body, liquids, aspirin, Tylenol (10)
Mal de estomago (8) (upset stomach)	something eaten (8)	fast 1 or 2 days (8)
	worms (8)	medication (8)
	weather (2)	protect body (1)
		uncertain (1)
Calentura (13) (fever)	weather (13)	analgesic (13)
	winds (13)	analgesic (13)
	injection (10)	analgesic (13)
Catarro (12) (head cold)	weather (5)	analgesic, cough syrup if needed (12)
	uncertain (7)	
Dolor de los Pulmones (3)		
Tuberculosis (3)	uncertain (2)	medication (2)
	infection (1)	medication (1)
	weather (1)	medication (1)
Pneumonia (1)	weather (1)	medication (1)

Table 3.1--continued

Illness	Cause	Cure
Weakness (7)		
Children (4)	weak blood (4)	vitamins and iron (2) no cure (1) uncertain (1)
Adults (4)	worms (4) weak or low blood (5)	medication (4) vitamins and iron (4) uncertain (1)
	worms (4)	medication (4)
Lombrises (5)		
Children (5)	eating worms (5)	medication (5)
Adults (4)	eating worms (3) uncertain (1)	medication (4)
Muscular pains (4)	physical strain (4)	liniment (3) uncertain (1)
Pesticide poisoning (2)	tactile contamination (2)	medication (2)
Varicose veins (1)	uncertain (1)	uncertain (1)
Cancer (2)	from Satan (1) uncertain (1)	uncertain (2)

the pre-Columbian beliefs. According to this model, health represents a state of internal bodily equilibrium, of being neither hot nor cold. Illness indicates a state of disequilibrium which may be the result of neglecting the inherent humoral "temperature" qualties of some item ingested or touched, or the psychological or emotional state resulting from a particular experience of event.

According to this model, cure requires discovering the cause of the imbalance to confirm the diagnosis, and restoring equilibrium. Prevention of illness requires careful considerations in not upsetting the balance. Among Guatemalan peasants it has been observed that belief in the humoral qualities serves as fundamental principle that guides daily behavior, influencing the individual's diagnosis of illness, choice of appropriate treatment and assessment of treatment outcome (Logan:1973a).

Although adoption of the underlying philosophy of humoral beliefs was far-reaching throughout the region following the Conquest, the degree of shared knowledge or agreement, the pervasiveness of the idiom, or its cultural importance vary considerably from place to place. Probable factors affecting this include how well and completely the ideas were transmitted and recieved given the absence of written records, tempered by memory, geographic and social isolation, and practical experience through generations of

illness and healing episodes (Adams and Rubel, 1967).
Perhaps the most thorough documentation of the hot-cold
syndrome in Mesoamerica is that of the humoral
classification of foods. Such a classification identifies
specific rules or guidelines for food selection in health
care during illness, especially under conditions of
physiological stress, such as pregnancy, illness, and old
age.

A comparison of qualties ascribed to certain foods in
various Guatemalan communties expose some of the
similarities and differences, and changes in the hot-cold
classifications through time and exposure to modern medical
practices. Various authors have noted some new concepts,
such as fresco, alimento , "strong" foods and concepts such
as "growth promoting" foods (Logan, 1973a; Gonzalez, 1964;
Cosminsky, 1975). Indeed, Cosminsky (1975) suggests that
the use of these new concepts, especially in areas in close
proximity to urban areas, indicated that the traditional
framework of illness prevention, causation and treatment are
being syncretized with modern concepts of health, largely a
result of the educational efforts of health care agencies.

Guatemalans in Indiantown have brought with them some
beliefs and perceptions of health and illness based on the
humoral model. In Indiantown, the Community Health Center
cites those complaints related to diarrhea (diarrea) and

fever (calentura) as the most common among their Guatemalan
clientele, especially for the children. Gatemalan families
concur. A primary focus of public health measures, diarrhea
and related complications have been identified as the major
causes of infant and child mortality in Guatemala (Mata,
1978:163; Logan, 1973b). The influence of public health
programs is evident as all refugees interviewed mentioned
"bad" or dirty water as a cause of diarrhea, and most people
said that they did not a drink tap water unless it is
boiled. Nonetheless, most refugee mothers expect that their
children, especially infants, will have bouts of diarrhea on
and off for years.

Those ailments most likely to be attributed to either
excessive heat are diarrhea and calentura. Mothers complain
that of the main cause of diarrhea in Indiantown is
excessive heat, generally referring to the weather. This is
considered by the Guatemalans to be "simple" diarrhea
because there is no evidence of blood or worms in the feces.
Treatment includes drinking cool water (that has been
boiled) to drink, but Kool Aid or Gatorade are preferred.
These are "cooling" drinks. In the event of possible
diarrhea inducing hot weather, the child may be stripped
down to his diapers and kept out of the sun, or even placed
in front of electric fans to keep cool.

Also in accordance with the classical humoral model,
any sudden change, be it hot-to-cold or cold-to-hot, is also
to be avoided. Essentially, it is the same problem of
extremes. Any such change would not promote an equilibrium,
but will only create a new imbalance. One mother recalled
that her baby became very sick after a nurse attempted to
wash her soiled by placing the his body in a sink under a
faucet of what appeared to the mother to be running cold
water. According to the mother, the infant, who was
suffering with a bout of diarrhea at the time only became
more ill as a result.

Concerns and practices relating to weather conditions,
especially temperature, may be viewed as adaptive responses
to environmental conditions. For example, McCullough (1973)
suggests that the hot-cold syndrome among the Yucatecan Maya
is an important aspect of biocultural adaptation to thermal
stress. In particular, the hot-cold syndrome in the Yucatan
dictates physiologically realistic rules for behavior during
work in a hot climate. According to the Yucatecan beliefs,
the three basic rules especially useful in prevention of
heatstroke and heat cramps are a water-salt rule, a cold
exposure rule, and a work pacing rule (McCullough:33-34).
Clearly, these rules are very pragmatic.

Some refugee mothers will wait for two or three days
before taking action for "simple" diarrhea because it is

thought that it will eventually abate without interference.
Given that many common illnesses are indeed self-limiting,
this again may be considered a pragmatic response based on
previous experience. At seven month's, Maria's son
developed a case of "simple" diarrhea that did not go away.
After a couple of days she took him to the Health Center and
was instructed to make sure the child drank plenty of
Gatorade and other liquids. After nearly two years of
almost continual diarrhea and repeated visits to the Health
Center, Maria's son suddenly got better because, according
to her, he finally got used to the hot weather in
Indiantown. The clinica nurse suggested that most probably
the mother continued to feed the child milk or formula
during this time which only aggravated the condition.

Diarrhea among older children and adults is not
perceived as being as much of a major concern although
intestinal pains or upset stomachs (mal de estomago) are
discussed in reference to diarrhea. Unlike the "simple"
diarrhea frequently experience by infants and small
children, the symptoms of mal de estomago may be brought on
by either cold or hot weather or by something that was
ingested that does not agree with the organism.

While it is believed that certain foods may cause the
symptoms associated with mal de estomago this may not
necessarily related to any beliefs about their inherent

temperature.   Rather, the foods mentioned that have caused
mal de estomago are spicy Mexican foods, too much fried
meat, and milk, and all were described as being not
tolerated by body. The ability to tolerate these foods is a
highly individual matter, and not generalized to any group
in particular.   In general, however, people note that all
excesses are to be avoided to prevent the problem.   Since
many herbs that might be used to cure diarrhea and mal de
estomago in Guatemala are not available in Florida, most
agreed that the best solution is to refrain from eating or
drinking anything for a day or two.

Calentura is often used to mean both high temperature
(temperatura) and fever (fiebre).   It is determined in
infants and children as well as adults by feelng the face
and neck to check if it is unusually warm.   All those
interviewed stated that this condition is caused by some
extreme, either hot or cold, again relating primarily to
weather.   In one case, however, a four year old boy had
calentura as a result of drinking an entire two-litre bottle
of soda (a "cold" drink). Symptoms that are perceived to
accompany calentura include loss of appetite and
irritability. Calentura that provokes diarrhea, however, may
also be a sign of someting more serious, most likely
requiring medical attention.

A newborn infant exposed to cool drafts of wind or too much direct sun may become ill with calentura. To prevent this, mothers will try to keep the infant in a closed and protected room. Upon entering a room where a newborn is kept, the sensation is that of a very stuffy and warm environment. Windows and doors are covered with sheets and blankets, and the child will be placed strategically at the point furthest from danger. Infants who have to be taken out, either for an appointment at the Health Department or for some other reason, are always well protected by layers of wrappings with a well covered head. Mothers who have to leave their children with baby-sitters often complain that not enough care is taken in this respect.

Injections may also cause calentura. Mothers note that health workers warn them that the vaccinations the child receives may cause a fever. The nurses also tell the mothers that if the child has been recently ill, or has a temperature, he can not be given a vaccination until he is recovered. All refugee mothers interviewed said that it would be dangerous to give the child more calentura than what he already has, and they will refrain from vaccinating if the child has been ill with a fever. The mothers are aware that the fever can be treated with Children's Tylenol and this is the preferred treatment among the Guatemalan

families interviewed.   All households with small children
had at least one bottle of this remedy on hand.

Adults may also get _calentura_, with the same symptoms
as children and infants and diagnosed in a similar manner.
Again, the most common cause is related to the weather, be
it too hot or too cold.   The Guatemalan refugees believe
that pregnant, lactating and menstruating women have a
higher risk for _calentura_.   Gonzalez (1969) and Cosminski
(1975) have noted that these altered states have humoral
implications in other Guatemalan populations.   Gonzalez
suggests that this is a time when the woman's body is
unusually "hot" (1969:221), while Cosminski says that this
is when the woman is weak, and, consequently is "cold"
(1975:189).

Guatemalan women in Indiantown did not express that
menstruation or pregnancy was a time when the woman was
particularly hot or cold. Often, a woman will wear a bandana
on her head, for example, but some say that it is to keep
from getting cold, while others say it is to prevent from
getting too hot. For the same reasons, women working in the
fields and orchards will also wear bandanas to protect their
heads from the sun, and men will wear hats.

It is perceived that those who are weak or lack
strength (_debil_ or _no tiene mucha fuerza_) tend to be ill
more frequently than those who are stronger, but this is not

the cause of illness. Again, this concurs with Cosminski's
observation of the belief that weak persons are more
susceptible. For example, a common belief based on this
perception is that a menstruating women who gets calentura
probably neglected to protect herself from adverse weather
conditions, the actual cause of illness.

The general malaise catarro, sometimes translated as a
head cold, does not have a single determining characterisitc
but rather encompasses any combination of various symptoms
including temperature, cough, sore throat, and sinus pain.
There was also less certainty about what causes catarro.
The symptoms are treated with over-the-counter analgesics,
again primarily aspirin or Tylenol for the temperature, and
cough drops or syrups for the others. No adults interviewed
sought medical assistance for catarro, either for themselves
or their children. However, three single men, during the
census interview, revealed that they had visited the Health
Center for the treatment of catarro and the flu-like gripe.

Among the more debilitating and diseases that are
perceived by some of the Guatemalans as prevalent in
Indiantown are tuberculosis, sometimes described as dolor de
los pulmones (pain in the lungs), and intestinal parasites.
Dolor de los pulmones may also mean pneumonia, and because
they share many similar symptoms, few people could describe
the difference between tuberculosis and pneumonia

(<u>pulmonia</u>). Pneumonia is believed to be more dangerous with
more severe symptoms which include fever and heavy coughing
with mucus.   Pneumonia is considered more of a problem is
mountainous regions with cold air, and is not a problem for
those in Indiantown.

Tuberculosis may occur anywhere in any kind of weather.
Sometimes the tuberculosis may not be recognized as such,
but rather may be confused with other muscular pains
resulting from the physical stress of farm work.   For
example, the manifest symptoms may only be upper back pain,
accompanied by shallow breath and general weakness.   At
least eight adult Guatemalans in Indiantown have been
diagnosed with tuberculosis and many are receiving
treatment.   There is little doubt that there are may be
several undiagnosed cases.   Tuberculosis is seen primarily
as an adult disease of unsure etiology.   Of course, the
danger according to health professionals lies in not
recognizing the symptoms at all. Of the three persons who
named tuberculosis as a problem one has been diagnosed with
the disease in Arizona and is still receiving treatment.   He
was somewhat more informed than the others, was able to
describe the tuberculosis and explain the dangers of not
receiving treatment, including contagion, according to the
bio-medical model.

WEAKNESS AS A CAUSE OF ILLNESS

Not all illnesses may be caused by an imbalance of hot
and cold elements. An alternate theme of binary opposites
characterizes a model of strength and weakness as a cause of
health and illness. Whether or not one is considered strong
or weak may be defined by one's history, and not so much
with the present situation. Thus, a child or adult may be
considered to be strong because they have survived well some
past hardships or illness even though the present situation
may not reflect this. Parents tend to be less worried about
the health status of their older children who were born in
Guatemala and made the trip to Florida without major
problems. Indeed, many children were left behind in Mexico
and Guatemala with other family members, often because it
was feared that they might not be able to survive the trip.
"Acquired weakness", however, is only a temporary condition
and may even befall a strong person. Cosminski (1975) also
notes a similar belief in Santa Lucia Utatlan as further
evidence of the syncretization of the biomedical and
indigenous theories of health and illness.

In this model, strength is positively correlated with
the good quality and quantity of one's blood. Because the
body's blood supply is viewed as a limited supply, taking
blood samples, even if from a finger prick, may be a very

anxiety provoking experience, especially for pregnant and postpartum women, and their newborns. Some women, however, believe that it is a risk worth taking because the nurses are able to tell them whether or not there is something wrong with their blood. Since all mothers in this sample are currently participating in the WIC program, it is not certain to what extent this notion has been influenced or modified by the practices of taking blood samples for the testing of hemoglobin levels and hematocrits in some of the public health programs in which the women may have participated, past or present .

A main concern among the Guatemalans is that the mother's or child's blood may be bajo (low) or debil (weak). Some women also call this condition anemia (anemia), the term generally learned at a health facility either in Indiantown or elsewhere. There is apparently no clear conceptual distinction between low and weak blood, and sometimes the terms are interchanged.

It is believed that one may be born with the condition or it may be the result of excessive blood loss during menstruation or during the birthing process. Women report that this is diagnosed by the nurse who can see if there is iron in the blood, but one can also tell if the blood is "low" if blood does not come out when the finger is pricked.

The color of one's blood is also an indicator of its quality. Menstruating women in particular are concerned about the color of their menstrual blood. A pinkish color is an indication of "weak" blood, but a very dark red or "almost black" blood is also a sign of an irregularity and cause for concern. The causes of these symptoms and what they might mean are not certain, and most women state that they would go to a doctor or clinic for these conditions if exagerated. Home treatment includes abdominal and lower back massages with oil, a traditional Mayan curing procedure. If an experienced woman or midwife is present, she may also feel for the uterus to see if the woman is pregnant, in which case the uterus would feel firm and shaped like a small apple. If there is no pregnancy, the uterus would be soft.

As opposed to an inherent weakness, since an "acquired weakness" is considered to be only temporary, prescriptions for it cure do exist. All women interviewed reported that the treatment for "acquired weakness" or "low" blood includes "eating iron." Apparently influenced by misconstrued interpretations of WIC recommendations, mothers said that foods that have iron are juices like those obtained through WIC, and meat. In addition, some men and women noted that weaknes may be helped by taking vitamins.

ILLNESSES CAUSES BY THINGS INGESTED

One illness already discussed in relation to adverse thermal conditions, mal de estomago, may also be caused by food eaten that is disagreable, resulting in symptoms like stomach aches, cramping and perhaps diarrhea. Another health problem is caused by the ingestion of worms and other microbios (microbes). The suspected high prevalence of intestinal parasites on the part of the health workers in Indiantown is, for the most part, shared by the refugees.

Children may infect themselves with lombrisis, or gusanitos (worms) when they play in the dirt and subsequently eat the worms in the filth. It is believed that the worms grow inside of the body, living off of the child's blood, thereby making him weak. They may also cause diarrhea and suspicious parents can see if the child has worms by inspecting his stools. Most parents, however, warn their children not to play with dirty things or in certain areas. Indeed, one woman was quite adamant in claiming that her four year old child had not eaten any worms, but agreed that younger children are more difficult to supervise, always putting things in their mouths.

Adults are somewhat reluctant to admit that they may have intestinal parasites of any kind. Most often, if abdominal pains are persistent and there is no evidence of

worms in the feces, adults will self-diagnose as having mal
de estomago and will treat accordingly.   However, if no
relief occurs after a reasonable (undetermined) time, the
patient will go to be diagnosed in a clinical setting, and
receiving   medication   is   then   considered   appropriate
treatment by the Kanjobal for the infected, or "invaded"
individual.   However, many treatments involve the entire
household taking medication as a precaution.   This raises
the question, and indeed problem of compliance as such
precautionary therapy is not considered necesary.

FOOD HABITS AND HEALTH

There is a great deal of uncertainty expressed by
Kanjobal women and men regarding how vitamins, calcium and
iron can be in foods, how they can be eaten, and the link
between these substances, their consumption and the quality
and quantity of one's blood.   There appear to be some
beliefs   based   on   misconceptions   of   nutritionists'
recommendations. For example, the belief that WIC fruit
juices contain iron may have arisen as a result of
recommendations to serve the juices along with the iron
fortified cereals or in the general meal plan to insure iron
absorbtion aided by the vitamin C inthe juices. One woman,
expressing her doubts, commented that iron is a very strong

substance ("el hiero es muy fuerte") and that that is why
the nurses recommend it, but she was unsure as to how it
could be in the foods she ate.

Unlike ethnographic reports on the Guatemalan humoral
classification of foods, in Indiantown the Guatemalans do
not follow any specific food selection rules based on this
classification. Foods in general do not appear to have any
particular beneficial properties other than the belief that
if it tastes good and does not cause an upset stomach, it
must be good for you as well. Indeed, this has been to the
dispair of WIC nutritionist and the dentist who note a large
proportion of calories consumed from candies, soft drinks,
potato chips, and other "junk food." Candies and sweets,
however, are perceived to give strength (da fuerza) but only
temporarily, while a good meal, which includes two to four
tortillas and some meat, "fills the stomach." A major
exception to this is the knowledge that milk promotes
growth and good health, but will be avoided is not well
tolerated.

The Guatemalans consume a wide variety of foods, and
are open to experimenting with new or novel foods. Learning
new forms of food preparation, and personal taste
preferences may hinder adoption of some new foods. However,
questions regarding beliefs about the role of particular
foods in health care require further investigation. Some

bias in this data on beliefs related to food presented herein may have resulted from the fact that I have worked extensively during the WIC "Guatemalan Wednesdays," and that I often translated for my informants on these occassions. Therefore, although through extensive participant observation, including accompanying families when shopping and sharing their meals, I was able to observe what is actually eaten, my informants may have tried to impress upon me that they understood WIC recommendations.

SUPERNATURAL CAUSES OF ILLNESS

There is little doubt that the role of therapeutic practices of traditional curers throughout the world has been affected by the availability and success of modern medical practices (Landy, 1974). San Miguel and surrounding areas have received medical assistance from Maryknoll priests for the last twenty years. A missionary hospital in the town of Jacaltenango, the largest administrative center near San Miguel, remains the only major medical facility in the area. It also sponsors a community health program for promotores de salud (health promotors) under the Catholic diocese of Dios es Sano ("God is Health"). The promotores are trained to help the communities where they work overcome some of their public health problems through projects and

health education.   Most of the refugees have received
immunizations or first aid from such promotores at one time
or another.

Although these promotores have received training in
working with indigenous healers in Guatemala, they claim
that it is very difficult if not impossible to coordinate
efforts.   For the most part, they realize that these health
caretakers operate under a different system, particularly in
the case of witchcraft, or brujeria.

The belief in supernatural causes of illness in
pre-Columbian Guatemala (Orellana, 1977), modified by and
adapted to elements of Catholic mysticism, is considered one
of the major sources of explanation of illness throughout
the Guatemalan highland region.   According to the
promotores, and supported by other refugees, brujos are not
very common anymore, whereas every family knows at least one
curandero (curer).   The health promotor movement, however,
as a program of the   Catholic Action movement was linked
with the conscious destruction of costumbre and the
compulsory surrender of the traditional household shrines
and idols used in traditional curing practices in exchange
for promotor health care services.   It has thus been
suggested that in Momostenango,

"in the development of of the
alternative catechism, the good/evil and

> spiritual/material dualisms were shifted
> from an external opposition between
> Christianity and witchcraft . . . to an
> internal complementarity within a
> religion and a pantheon that encompass
> the Chrisitan divinities rather than
> opposing them" (Tedlock, 1982:43)

In Indiantown, four people interviewed expressed some belief in witches. One couple, interviewed at a time when headcolds and diarrhea were widespread among the younger children in Blue Camp, did express some suspicion that the recent refugee arrivals might have been responsible for causing the wave of illness. One explained that they brought the illnesses with them, while the other suggested that they gave the illness because of jealousy toward Guatemalans already living there who had acquired things like automobiles and televisions. However, this was the only case when witchcraft was ever mentioned as a cause of illness, or when it was hinted that an illness could be caused by psychological or emotional states like jealousy.

One thirty-two year old woman, when asked if there were brujos in Indiantown, stated that there probably were not because of the absence of landmarks or evil places in town where malevolent forces would gather. This corresponds to beliefs in the Mayan village in the Chiapas highlands of Mexico where spirits with powers to inflict misfortune and illness are associated with places and landmarks (Nash, 1970:11-26).

One other woman, an Adventist, was more concerned with diseases caused by Satan (Satanas), particularly cancer, not that she knew of anyone who had cancer, but that this was an illness believed to be sent as a punishment to the infidel.

"NEW" ILLNESSES

Up to this point, the illnesses perceived as problematic in Indiantown have been the same, or similar, to some of those with which the refugees have had some experience in Guatemala. Their etiologies, symptoms and cures remain "logical" within in a conceptual framework. The new environment and lifestyle have brought along some new illnesses, however, which not seem to fit into any such familiar model. People do not recognize many of the symptoms and cannot make a certain diagnosis. These are "new" or novel illnesses and often the refugees find out about them from health workers, other non-Guatemalan co-workers and neighbors.

Among the work related illnesses is the growing fear of pesticide and herbicide poisoning. Through efforts of the Service Center and the farm labor union, information about the threat of pesticide poisoning for those who work in the fields is being disseminated throughout the community. Because many of the work codes are not being enforced, or because workers are not well informed, however, cases of poisoning have continued to develop. One Guatemalan man whose neck, upper chest and arms had the appearance of a severe eczema and burns came first to the Service Center desparate for help. He had the condition for several days before coming and self-treated by applying kalamine lotion every morning and evening, following the advice of a Mexican co-worker. However, the discomfort only increased. He thought that perhaps he got the ailment from his clothes that, at one point, were handled by a black woman in the laundromat. He was taken to the health center and was assured that the burns were chemically induced, probably by a pesticide.

Among the women, the new concerns are urinary tract infections (UTI) and vaginitis. It has been suggested by a nurse that if the women did not wear tight pants, especially when pregnant, the incidence of UTI and vaginitis would decline dramatically. Women who work in the fields and feel awkward about using the available sanitation facilities, or do not know where they are, are also particularly vulnerable. Even though no one interviewed had ever had these illness prior to leaving Guatemalan, women who have developed UTI in Indiantown and received treatment are very articulate regarding the symptoms. Many are also able to describe it as an infection that may damage the kidneys.

Vaginitis, however, remains somewhat more of a mystery because the symptoms and cause tend to be more obscure and is diagnosed only during pre-natal check-ups or during the family planning examination.

NEW REMEDIES VERSUS OLD REMEDIES

Many of the illnesses preceived as problematic require some kind of medication. The most common remedies found in the homes include over-the-counter analgesics, cough syrups and drops, and liniment for aching muscles. Some women may have pre-natal vitamins or iron supplements if they had been recommended by a nurse. All homes with small children have a bottle of Children's Liquid Tylenol. These are considered very expensive medicines and not especially potent. Guatemalan medicines are considered to be about the same or better than American medicines. No one suggested that American medicines were superior. Greater confidence in and familiarity with the effects of medicines and other remedies from Guatemala has resulted in what appears to be their increasing presence in Indiantown. These remedies are brought, often by request, by recent arrivals, friends and family. Among these are injections and herbs that are not available in Indiantown.

One of the puzzles expressed by the refugees is why the doctors in the United States do not give injections, but rather prescribe expensive pills. Injections are perceived as clearly more effective and more potent than any pills. For example, refugee mothers are very keen to have their children immunized knowing that it will keep them from getting illnesses that are very serious. However, medication for injections brought from Guatemala are also expensive, even if they are paid for with dollars with some paying ten to twenty dollars each. This is especially unfortunate because they will not be able to find anyone in Indiantown qualified to give the injections. The promotor states that he has been asked several times to administer such injections but has been telling people that he cannot do so legally. Instead, he advises them to consult a doctor for their complaints. At the time of this investigation, although some people have the medicines, no one claims to have received an injection.

Unlike vaccinations which are believed to prevent the incidence of illness, these injections are said to be beneficial for giving strength, with one major exception that is reportedly used to induce miscarriage. The bottles are poorly labeled, if labeled at all, making their identification difficult. It was explained that the way to get them in Guatemala is to present one's symptoms or name

of the illness to a pharmacist who will then prescribe the
appropriate medicine.   It is suspected that if these were
readily available in most any pharmacy in Guatemala, and
given their purported qualities, they may be antibiotics
such as penicillin, or vitamins, such as vitamins B or C.
Their perceived potency and effectiveness is understandable
since injections introduce the medication more immediately
into the blood stream than those orally introduced.

Other remedies that have found their way to Indiantown
are various herbs (hierbas). Of the four kinds I saw, only
chamomile (manzanilla) and another, actually from Mexico,
hierba buena, were identified.   These two are considered to
have curative qualities and as teas are useful for mal de
estomago and catarro.   These are both listed in Logan's
(1973b) account of plant medicinals used for digestive
disorders. No one interviewed was aware that both of these
herbs are availale in the local markets, however. The other
two are used for cosmetic purposes, including making the
hair shiney and for promoting a good complexion.   The woman
using these herbs either did not know any name for them, did
not know the Spanish equivalent or were sufficiently
embarrassed about having them to not want to identify the
names.

The Guatemalans have had contact with and been
influenced by other hispanic groups since leaving their

homeland, particularly the Mexicans. Most Guatemalans in Indiantown have daily interaction with Mexicans and Puerto Ricans through work, and some have shared housing. Mexican music and style of clothing are particularly admired by the Guatemalans. It is not unlikely that this influence may also apply to other areas, including health.

Some specific cases indicate that there have been changes in some behaviors in particular households, but these are not general to most households. For example, Maria's family lived with a Mexican family from Michoacan for five months in Indiantown. She learned to prepare several Mexican foods, and she also followed the example of her housemates by serving cheese to the children at meals. Cheese is one of the foods available through the WIC program, but is generally not very popular among the Guatemalans, primarily as a result of taste and custom. Maria saw that it did not harm the Mexican children, and so decided that since she could get it at no cost through WIC, she would serve ot to the children. She also encouraged her cousin to do the same for her children. It is interesting to note that none of the women nor their husbands care for the taste or texture of the cheese and do not eat it.

A willingness to experiment with new ways and seek advice of others especially among the young single people is illustrated by the experiences of Candelaria. One day I

went to visit Juana, one of eighteen year old Candelaria's
house mates. When I knocked on the door to her apartment it
was opened, but whoever opened it did not show her face.
When I entered the room I was surprised that Candelaria was
home and not at work.   I immediately noticed that
Candelaria's face was covered with a dark brown paste. At
first she did not want to discuss the strange mask. She
explained that she stayed home to watch the apartment
because Juana was going to be gone all day. After a while
she laughed and confessed that a Mexican girl friend had
told her that the cream would help to remove the dark
(sunburn) patches on her cheeks.   The cream was made of
melted dark chocolate with salt added and was to be left on
the face for several hours.   Candelaria was not sure it
would work, but thought it was worth a try anyway. The same
friend on a previous occasion had advised her on a special
shampoo that was responsible for her long, straight hair.
Similarly, Diego, who had pesticide poisoning, followed the
advice of his Mexican co-worker and used Kalamine lotion for
several days before seeking medical attention.

        Families that attend services at a Seventh Day
Adventist church in West Palm Beach are particularly
influenced by Cubans and Cuba-Americans as well as Puerto
Ricans who worship at the same church. Mothers with their
small children are separated from the rest of the

congregation in a sound-proof room at the entrance of the church, behind the pews, so that they can nurse and supervise their youngest childen.   Much information is exchanged during the three hour long service, as well as gossip. On one of these occassions Micaela received advice on how to treat her varicose veins, and how to best care for her baby's birthmark.

In all of these cases, the Guatemalans spoke sufficient Spanish and had long term relationships with Mexicans who befriended them and were considered trustworthy. The extent to which beliefs, percpetions and attitudes regarding health and illness have been influenced by contact with these other groups, however, is not certain. It may be surmised that with increased exchange of information between individuals and groups more profound changes will come about as the need arises, for example, when illness do not respond to the old curing practices, or in the case of "new" illnesses.

THE SICK ROLE

"It is necessary be healthy to work hard and earn money to live." This is the standard response by the refugees to the question "What does it mean to be healthy?" Illness prevents the individual from successful work performance, and when most people get paid by the amount of boxes or crates filled, being ill can mean a significant loss of income. A greater loss would be sustained if the individual does not work at all.

To be sick means that an illness has be diagnosed, either by that same person or a doctor, not going to work, staying at home or going to the health center for a consultation, and not bringing in any pay. For the head of a refugee family with two or three small children and perhaps a pregnant, unemployed wife the implications are clear. Being ill carries a stigma of weakness and an inability to carry out responsibilities. That is why many women and men will often complain of various aches and pains, but will go out to work day after day. A similar pattern is reported among Mexicans and Mexican-Americans (Clark, 1959; Madsen, 1964; Rubel, 1966). Sick children are expected to stay home from school.

The reluctance to accept the sick role can have serious consequences. In 1985, for example, Andres was diagnosed in Arizona as having tuberculosis. He moved to Indiantown shortly thereafter. He often complains of back and lung pains and weakness, and occasionally has <u>catarro</u>. He is currently supporting two children less than five years old and has another on the way. His wife brings in some extra cash by washing clothes by hand for their landlord neighbor, and receives WIC coupons. On at least two occassions Andres failed to appear at appointments to check on the tuberculosis even though transportation had been arranged. He had long ago stopped taking the medication given to him in Arizona because he did not like having to take the pills every day, and has since lost the remaining pills. Whether or not he fully understands the nature of tuberculosis and its debilitating effects is questionable, but there is no doubt that any steps beyond those already taken would require that he miss at least one day or work if not more because he is not on a contract, and if he really is sick, then he fears that the treatment may be too costly. When asking which are are the most problematic illnesses neither Andres nor his wife mentioned tuberculosis.

The sick role may also provide a desired excuse for not working as well. Angelina is a thirty-eight year old woman who had two miscarriages in Mexico before coming to Indiantown in 1983. After arriving, she began to have increasing abdominal pains and some bleeding (of uncertain origin, whether rectal or vaginal). During this time she continued working with her husband in the fields picking grapefruits, leaving her two pre-school children with her fifteen year old daughter. Once Angelina was considered too ill to work, her daughter (then fifteen years old) took her place at work, and Angelina stayed at home. In early 1986 after a very long and complicated procedure to check for possible ulcers or an ovarian cyst, and then subsequently diagnosed as having parasites, she began treatment for helminths. Angelina, however, has continued to stay at home even after her treatment for parasites was over. So long as her daughter continues to work, and does not get married, this is financially feasible for Angelina. Her husband says that she is still too weak to work, but Angelina adds in private that she does not like to work in the fields because it is too hard for her. As long as her daughter prefers to work in the fields to watching her younger siblings, Angelina does not plan on returning to work.

A similar comment was made by another young woman who constantly complains of pain in her uterus. Juana, a very shy and quiet woman, about nineteen years old, has been to see a doctor at the health center, once with a friend and once I took both her and her sister for consultation. She has had at least two pregnancy tests, each with negative results and has expressed concern that she may be infertile. Juana has also been seeing one of the Guatemalan midwives who has been unable to help her. However, Juana has never gone to see the fertility specialist referred to her by the doctor even though an appointment and transportation had been arranged with her consent. In the meantime, she continues to stay at home often spending time with a pregnant housemate. Since she has no children and her

husband is able to find jobs nearly every day, the financial
pressures are less than for other families.   Even so, her
husband considers her to be too weak to work in the fields,
and she is relieved.

GENERAL OBSERVATIONS

     Among Mesoamerican peasants in general, there are four
main models of illness and disease causation: illness as a
result of some natural injury or accident; the disruption of
the internal harmony of the body; the result of witchcraft
through activities by supernatural and human agents with
malevolent intentions; the presence of foreign objects or
organisms into the body (Logan, 1973b:183).   As we have
seen, what causes an illness will determine the appropriate
therapeutic response: a fever caused by too much heat must
be cooled down.   What causes an illness will also determine
if and how preventive measures may apply.   In addition, an
human ecological perspective may provide useful insights to
some beliefs and practices related to illness prevention.

     For most of the illnesses described by the Guatemalans,
few involve any contagion.   There is a some concept of
contagion, primarily in the case of intestinal parasites
that may be picked up from the environment, but not from
other individuals.   Prevention requires making sure that

dirt and dirty things are not injested. Things that may be spread from person to person by touch include lice, skin rashes, and some eye and ear infections. Diarrhea, calentura can be helped in most cases by watching the weather. Catarro, like diarrhea and fever, is also not generally considered to be contagious, but chickenpox and polio as well as other diseases for which the children are immunized are very contagious.

Among the Kanjobal women in Indiantown there appears to be little understanding of the role of foods in good nutrition, in the bio-chemical sense, and disease prevention even though many are able to parrot some of the nutritionists' recommemdations. In addition, the connection between fetal growth and good nutrition is not clearly understood. Of nine pregnant women interviewed, only one was able to identify the role of the umbilical cord in bringing nutrients to the fetus. One woman said that the fetus drinks the milk that the mother drinks and that is what makes it grow. Similarly, the reason pregnant women should not drink beer is that the fetus will choke on it and die.

Breast-feeding is considered to be good, but impractical for working mothers. When possible, the mother will give the breast, as a supplement, for as long as two or three years. The idea that some foods have more vitamins

than others and that vitamins are health promoting is
generally accepted, but the idea that foods contain
substances like iron, measured in hemoglobin readings,
remains suspect. The connection between food and blood is
also not clear.

This same conceptual "confusion" of how the body
functions may further explain why injections are preferred
to pills. Pills and other medication taken orally go to the
stomach and little is known about how they work from there.
One woman was concerned that she would gain weight if she
took birth-control pills for an extended period of time
because the pills would stay inside of her body. A similar
concern was expressed by the man who had to take
tuberculosis medication for a full year.

In general, the consensus among the refugees is that,
perhaps due to their improved lifestyles, primarily in terms
of eating more and better, there are fewer kinds of
illnesses and a decreased incidence of these in Indiantown,
and, by extension, in the United States. There are also
more doctors and nurses in Indiantown than most people are
used to and they are consulted whenever there is any doubt
that home treatment is not helping a situation.

Knowledge of the beneficial properties of basic
over-the-counter remedies such as aspirin and Children's
Tylenol is universal and is used appropriately when needed.

However, Guatemalan medicines and herbal remedies are often
perceived as superior, especially in terms of potency, and
are being brought to Indiantown at no small cost to the
refugees. This suggests that perhaps people are not feeling
as well, or as strong, as they think they should. This may
very well be the case considering that the majority of
adults and most children have not been screened for
intestinal parasites and that several varieties are endemic
to Indiantown as well as Guatemala and Mexico. If, as Logan
(1973b) suggests, the number of remedies available for a
particular ailment is indicative of its prevalence, then the
small sample of herbs witnessed in Indiantown may be
indicative of a special concern for disorders of the
digestive tract

     It is evident that this group of Guatemalans has been
considerably influenced by certain Western medical practices
and medicines for some time. Among these are immunizations,
blood sampling and injections. It is clear that some of the
native theories of health and illness have been modified or
syncretized even though doctors and hospitals were out of
reach for many of them in Guatemala. The system of promotor
de salud helped to fill many needs along with the local
pharmasists and herbalists. With the absence of traditional
healers in Indiantown, with the exception of midwives, and
given that the Guatemalans recognize that they are in a very

different environment from their homeland where there are
many things they do not yet understand, people are seeking
advice from those perceived to have relevant and reliable
knowledge. These include co-workers and friends, Service
Center volunteers, as well as nurses and doctors. Indeed,
almost invariably, the same questions were asked back to me!

CHAPTER FOUR
HEALTH RESOURCES AND BEHAVIOR

This chapter will discuss various factors that affect
the Guatemalan refugees' perceptions of the health care
resources they use, and explore some ways in which these
have influenced their understanding of health and illness
and their health-seeking behavior.

The notion of a career as a progression of events has
been used to order the elements of health-seeking behavior
in a natural sequence corresponding to various stages
through which an individual may pass during an illness
episode (McKinlay, 1975). These stages are generally
described as symptom recognition, lay referral,
self-medication, adoption of the sick role, and formal
therapeutic encounters. As discussed in the previous
chapter, the definition of health and illness, and
health-related beliefs of disease etiology and illness
prevention provide the background against which the career
is followed.

The "career" is not necessarily a linear progression
from one stage to the next, but rather may be influenced by
various mediatory factors, including the individual's
hierarchy of needs, interference in the normal course of

97

activities, accessibility of health care resources, and the
changing patterns of health problems as the perceived degree
of severity increases or decreases with time. These factors
may   be   viewed   as   constraints   and   built   into   a
decision-making   model   useful   for   predicting   the
health-seeking behavior of groups given certain conditions
(Young, 1980) and in cases of dual use (Press, 1969), the
concurrent use of a physician and a curer for treatment, and
hierarchy of resort (Romanucci-Schwartz, 1969), the order in
which a patient choses such treatment.

        Differential use of health resources may be also be
influenced by the perceived quality of the doctor-patient
relationship, and degree of patient satisfaction.   The
fulfillment of social needs (Hauser, 1981), the personal
characteristics of the physician (Klein, 1976), and the
degree to which the curer's performance corresponds to the
patient's expectations (Low, 1983) have been shown to
influence the patient's satisfaction with medical care.

EL CORTE AND LA CLINICA

        All of the Guatemalan families interviewed who had been
in Indiantown for at least six months were able to identify
the locations of both the Health Department, the _corte_, and
the Health Center, the _clinica_.   All described the major

difference between the two as the absence of a doctor and a dentist in the Health Department. Some people also noted that there are no male health workers in the corte, and the presence of male doctors in the clinica.

For refugee families, the most important services offered at the Health Department are considered to be the WIC program, immunizations, and family planning. Problems resulting from injuries, complaints of diarrhea, other digestive tract disorders, fever, and head cold, and the need for dental attention bring people to the Health Center. Family planning services also attract some refugee women to the Health Center. At the time of this study both facilities had bilingual receptionists, but all other health workers had very limited knowledge of Spanish, if any.

Both facilities are well respected for their services and the Guatemalans are generally satisfied with them. Due to the later operating hours of the Health Center, it is accessible to more families. If a mother's knowledge of Spanish is limited, or if she does not want to make the trip alone during the day, she must either wait for her husband to return from work, and they may then go together, or arrange to go with a friend more fluent in Spanish. If both parents work, the evening hours are indispensible.

Although the Guatemalans complain that they pay thirty to thirty-five dollars fee for Health Center services, it is not really considered unreasonable. This reflects the comparison that is often drawn between the expensive medical care in the United States and the free medical care available in Guatemala and Mexico where injections, the preferred form of medication, are given.

FAMILY PLANNING

Family planning has apparently gained in popularity and acceptability among the Guatemalan refugees, men and women, over the last few years. At least three women who, one year previously did not think that it was a good idea, are now using some form of birth control. Half of the women interviewed said that there is birth control, meaning the Pill, in Guatemala, and others said that it is not available. None of the women interviewed had ever used any form of contraceptive before coming to Indiantown.

In the case of family planning the clinica may be preferred to the corte, even though no fee is charged in the Health Department. The reasons given are two-fold. One is that women claim that the waiting time at the clinica is much less than at the corte, a conclusion often reached after experiences with other programs there which will be discussed in the following section.

The second reason is not totally unrelated to the first. The concern among Guatemalan women and couples for privacy and discreetness when seeking family planning is a problems in the Health Department strategy of having classes for the women on Tuesdays, the designated family planning clinic day. At this time not only do the women find out who else is seeking family planning, but Tuesday is widely known as the day when women go to the corte for their "pills." Women who do not wish that their husbands or other friends or relatives know that they are pursuing birth control, fearing disapproval, are thus risking discovery. In general, the Health Center offers more confidentiality.

The differential patterns in use of family planning service among the Guatemalans would seem to correspond to those of described by Scrimshaw (1978) among hispanized women in Latin America. Primarily, the strongest predictor for use of some birth control method in Scrimshaw's study and in Indiantown is a joint husband and wife decision. Refugee couples seeking birth control generally already have some children, and do not wish to have any more, at least for a while. The main reason given is financial.

However, the woman may exercize her decisions in areas that are not as obvious to the husband. These may be attempts at induced abortion when the husband is not present or using the most discreet of contraceptive means, namely,

the Pill. Unfortunately, there are problems with this
latter option although, unlike the diaphram and the foam and
condom, it is not only the most discreet but also most
passive contraceptive method. Most women who first seek
birth control are not aware that for the first month of
using the Pill they must also use one of the barrier methods
until the cycle has been regulated. This is often
distressing news to the woman, and one must wonder to what
extent these instructions are actually followed.

Some of the problems encountered in family planning are
illustrated in the following examples. One couple that came
together for family planning counseling returned in only two
weeks asking for more pills. The husband responded to all
the questions for his wife regarding how she felt, if she
was experiencing any irregular bleeding or pain, without
consulting her even though she did understand enough Spanish
to know what was being asked. She sat next to him silently
as he explained that apparantly the woman had taken two
pills a day, thinking that they work better if the dosage
was doubled. During the initial counseling, the husband
also responded to all the questions by the female nurse and
translator and stated that he understood the proceedures
required for use of the Pill. However, the subsequent visit
indicated that he did not fully understand why he had to

take extra precautions during the first few weeks, and that he had encouraged his wife to double the dosage.

In another case, Juana was taken off of the Pill after developing severe varicose veins. She did not opt to use another form of contraception because, she said, they were too difficult to use and her husband was not understanding. Within two months she was pregnant. At the time of this study, Juana was considering a tubal ligation after the birth of this last child.

As in Scrimshaw's study, the results from this study indicate that the older the woman, the greater the use of contraceptives and abortion. Scrimshaw suggests that this correlates with their greater autonomy in the family during later life stages (1978:51). At least one Guatemalan woman has had an abortion at a clinic in West Palm Beach only three months after the birth of her fourth child. Although she was relatively well informed, she neglected to seek some form of contraception following the birth of her last last child. It was estimated that this unwanted pregnancy occurred within the first month of the previous birth, and she did not think it possible for her to get pregnant again so soon after giving birth.

Considering the cost of being out of work for another extended period of time, and considering the physical cost, she sought advice on abortion. The woman was told of the clinic by an American friend. The woman was pleased with the painless procedure, but thought that it was very expensive ($200.00). Although she had the abortion with the consent of her husband, he did not pay for the abortion. She borrowed the money from various relatives in Indiantown explaining that her husband had incurred various debts that she was trying to pay. Soon thereafter she again expressed interest in sterilization.

Although induced abortion is not viewed positively by most of the Guatemalans, the presence of a supposed abortion-inducing medication brought from Guatemala suggests that in Guatemala it may occur with some frequency, albeit undetermined. Also, the behavior of at least one women who, during pregnancy, ate cigarrets and drank beer hints of an attempt to induce abortion. She was an older woman who had suffered three unsuccesful births in Guatemala and at least one previous miscarriage in rural Mexico. Following the successful birth of this last child in the hospital, she too asked for a tubal ligation.

Determining the reproductive histories of women proved to be difficult and unreliable for the reasons that some women did not want their husbands know of some terminated pregnancies. For those women who met their husbands since leaving Guatemala, their husbands often do not know about children they may have had by a previous relationship.

THE WOMAN, INFANT AND CHILD PROGRAM

The Woman, Infant, and Child (WIC) program, a supplemental nutrition and nutrition education program, is aimed at indigent pregnant and post-partum lactating women and infants and children under five years old certified as being at nutritional risk. WIC, housed in the Health Department on the second and fourth Wednesdays of the month for "Guatemalan Wednesday", is the health resource with the highest utilization rate among the Guatemalans for all eligible children up to five years of age as well as for pregnant women. Of the forty-two families eligible for WIC, all but one participated in it. This one family knew about the program but chose not to attend because they did not feel it was necessary.

The ways in which women participating in WIC found out about the program are listed in Table 4.1. The most common way for the Guatemalan women to find out about WIC is through the Service Center. Generally, during the course of a volunteer's normal daily activities, a newly arrived family would be "discovered" and informed, or the volunteer would advise a newly pregnant mother as to how to go about signing up for WIC. In the case where the women were referred by a friend or female relative, their informants were already WIC clients. Sometimes, the woman's husband

was the one to inform her after learning about it himself
either through a co-worker, relative or neighbor. He may
also have been informed by the Service Center. In the case
where the woman has a very limited understanding of Spanish,
and if there is no available female friend that is aleady
participating in WIC, the husband will accompany his wife to
the Health Department to help deal with the initial
paperwork. The other way that the mothers found out about
the program were through referrals from the Health Center or
from the Health Department as a result of pregnancy tests.
If the results were positive the women were given
appointments to certify for the program.

Table 4.1   How Guatemalan women find out about WIC.

Source	Number	%
Service Center	14	33
Friend/Female relative	9	21
Husband	7	17
Health Dept./Health Ctr.	7	17
Do not remember	4	9
Not known	1	2
Total	42	99

There is little doubt that the mothers value the
services of the WIC nutritionists and the nurses in the
Health Department. They are curious to know of their weight
gain during pregnancy, the quality of their blood, and of
the progress of their children. Many mothers also take the

opportunity during "Guatemalan Wednesday" to make sure that all immunizations are up to date for their children. The checks for infant formula are considered to be indispensible, especially for working mothers, as are the milk, eggs, juice, cheese and cereals for themselves and the older children. The savings on the monthly food budget could be as much as $47.00 for an infant, and $20 for a child.

There are two mutual concerns among both the Guatemalans and the WIC nutritionists. One of these is that of the proper use of the food received. The foods designated for a particular individual may be consumed by another family or household member, either as an economizing measure, or because of individual tastes and preferences. This is a problem not only restricted to the Guatemalan population, but indeed is manifested in all supplementary food programs (Dwyer, 1983; Underwood, 1983). Among those foods most likely to be discarded or given away are cheese, and milk. Milk is considered to be a healthy food and children in particular are encouraged to drink milk so that they may be strong. However, since many families have to share refrigerators, there may not be room enough for everyone's milk. There is a preference for fresh milk as opposed to powdered milk, especially during the warmer months, the milk left out will spoil before it can be used.

Cheese, on the other hand, is often discarded immediately after purchase, or given to someone, a friend or acquaintance who may use it. Because cheese is not a traditional food, one of foci of nutrition education classes has been to introduce ways of including cheese in traditional dishes. The problems with this have been that cheese, either the American style cheese slices or the block cheddar, is not liked by many because of the taste or the texture, especially by the adults. Some of the parents, however, do encourage the children to eat the cheese because "it has many vitamins." The Guatemalans complain that, contrary to the nutritionists' praises, milk and cheese cause stomach cramps and diarrhea (similar to mal de estomago). This suggests that, like many other Native American populations, they may be exhibiting signs of lactose intolerance. Whether or not this intolerance is due to lactase deficiency requires clinical verification.

The second major concern is also not unique to the Guatemalans, but concerns all indigent families participating in WIC. The problem is essentially a "Catch 22" in which the nutritionists are recommending the increased consumption of certain foods, such as meats, that may be prohibitive economically to many families, regardless of the assistance provided by WIC checks. Especially during the off-season, some women have expressed embarassment about having to do diet recalls for WIC because they have not been following recommendations. They will lie about their food habits, afraid that they will not receive their checks. When the lab results show that the woman may have lost weight, or that her hemoglobin reading is dangerously low, the nutritionist can only reiterate her recommendations, and perhaps recommend iron supplements.

"Guatemalan Wednesday" provides an opportunity for the women to socialize while in the waiting area, exchanging the latest gossip, information about where a certain product or object may be purchased, stories and observations about their children. Most working mothers will not go to work on these days, taking advantage of the fact that they have to pick up their checks to do some shopping, go to the post office or thrift store, or to go visiting. By the same token, however, there are some problems with this for some women who resent the relative lack of privacy during the certification and recertification procedure. This procedure is traced out step-by-step in Figure 4.1. Indeed, the building does not easily lend itself to this procedure, as the narrow hallway is the main route of both incoming and outgoing traffic, as well as the waiting space for those who need lab work done, or for a free consultation room. In addition, unless the office doors are closed, they afford little privacy in terms of sight or sound.

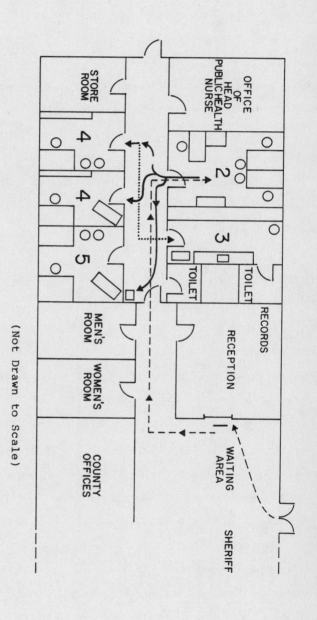

1 Sign in at Window
2 Clerks issue checks
3 Lab and Weight Scale
4 Consultation Rooms
5 Family Planning Room

Figure 4.1 Flow chart for WIC clinic, Indiantown

(Not Drawn to Scale)

Some working mothers maintain that half of the day is "wasted" waiting for the checks to be issued, and there is no time to do much else but go back home, and they have also lost a day's wages. If a woman comes early in the morning, she may have a half an hour's wait before being seen, and if a nutrition class is being offered first, this may take a bit longer, depending on the class. Then, it may take between five to ten minutes with the clerk for a recertification, perhaps five minutes longer for a certification. The lab work, including weighing an infant or child, takes about three to four minutes. The consultation with the nutritionist may be from two minutes to twenty. This wide variation often is a result of the nutritionist being called away during consultation to attend to other duties. The waiting between one step and the other may also vary from immediate attention to a fifteen minute wait. Thus, at worst, a woman may spend about two hours, and at best about forty minutes to complete the procedure. Thus, the amount of time spent for WIC is not predictable.

The WIC program is unique in that, unlike other food commodity programs, WIC includes a nutrition education component. The program goals are threefold: 1) the improvement of the nutrition and health status of participants as assessed by anthropometric and biochemical tests, and clinical observations; 2) to increase the participants' and parents' knowledge of nutritional needs and economic ways to meet those needs; and 3) effecting changes in food consumption habits toward more nutritionally adequate diets within family resources (DHRS, 1983:1-5, 1-6).

The nutrition education classes are expected to take place in a class-room setting ideally with all WIC clients present. The logistics problems encountered with this are many, including the lack of such a room, and the language barrier. Classes have been held in the waiting area and in the Sheriff Department's conference room. Even though there may be materials available in Spanish, the relatively low level of comprehension of Spanish in addition to the use of some concepts involved in nutrition unknown to the refugee women render most of the materials impractical. While some effort has been dedicated to translating a few of these materials into Kanjobal, much work remains. In the meantime, the non-Spanish speaking nutritionists must make do with what they can for classes, often depending on the occassion assistance from a Service Center volunteer to translate, and much more effort has been directed to individual counseling during the certification and recertification process.

None of the women interviewed mentioned the nutrition education as a positive aspect of the program. Indeed many women asked why classes were even held, and were even reluctant to participate. This raises a very important question as to how crucial is it to clearly state the goal of the program to clients. It appears that the goal of promoting beneficial food habits through increased knowledge of nutrition is not appreciated among the Guatemalan women. If this goal is not understood, WIC becomes little more than a food stamp program because receiving the checks becomes the primary purpose for participating, and the lab work and consultation are considered "fringe benefits," if not a duty to be performed in exchange for receipt of the checks.

The one family not participating in WIC expressed this attitude, maintaining that they only had one healthy new born and no other children to feed, and the husband had a good job. The fact that there are no doctors in the Health Department only supports this for the Guatemalans, the implication being that if this was a serious health program, doctors should be involved. This view is also consistent with the observation made in the previous chapter of this study that there is little conception of the biochemical aspects of nutrition as discussed by the nutritionists during classe and counseling and its role in illness prevention and good health.

Other potential constraints to going to the WIC clinic include getting to the Health Department safely, and the need to find someone to watch over the children that do not have to go and remain at home. Unless they can find a ride, the women walk to the Health Department, and except for those who live in the Booker Park area, they must walk along the shoulders of State Road 710, a road with constant automobile and truck traffic, and not safe for small children not well supervised. For those living in the Booker Park area the main concerns are the fear of being harassed by strangers, primarily black youths, and the fear of having the house burglarized during their absence, not an unrealistic fear as it does occur with great frequency. Nonetheless, given the success of the program to enroll eligible individuals, the benefits gained from WIC obviously outweigh most constraints.

THE IMPROVED PREGNANCY OUTCOME PROGRAM

Like WIC, the Improved Pregnancy Outcome (IPO) program is aimed at low income pregnant women. Through IPO fetal development and maternal health are monitored on a monthly basis throughout the duration of the pregnancy. Before May, 1986, the IPO program was held only in Stuart, and an attempt was made at scheduling all of the Guatemalan appointments on the same days to facilitate transportation and translator arrangements. However, as the number of Indiantown IPO patients climbed along with the number of missed apointments, the clinic has begun to operate once a week in Indiantown.

Unlike WIC, IPO has had a more difficult time recruiting and keeping clients coming in for regular appointments. IPO participants find out about the program primarily through the Health Department, being given an appointment to sign up following a positive pregnancy exam, or at the time of the WIC certification. Thus, all IPO clients are also WIC clients, but the reverse is not true.

The rate of utilization of IPO is difficult to assess due to two factors. One is that women may be enrolled in the program, but only attend the clinic sporadically, and as such do not consider themselves as clients of a "regular" program. The monthly exams, similar to the weigh-ins and hemoglobin checks performed at WIC, are not seen as part of a necessary cycle, especially if the expectant mother is not experiencing any difficulties in the pregnancy and is a WIC client. Transportation considerations also come into play to influence the decision not to go to Stuart. The second factor in utilization rates is the fact that many women do not enroll in the program until the pregnancy is quite advanced, sometimes as much as in the seventh or eighth

month. Since the time between enrolling in the program and
the first appointment is often a month, the birth may take
place before the first scheduled pre-natal check-up.

Women may wait this long before enrolling for two
reasons. The most common reason given for the delay is the
belief that if there are no difficulties, there is no need
to see a doctor, or to do any testing. However, as the
pregnancy advances, the mothers become more insecure and
decide to go to the clinic. The second reason for delaying
is the belief that hospital services will be denied if they
do not go to the clinic. One mother, for example, stated
that she was considering giving birth in the hospital in
Stuart, and was concerned that if she did not go to the
Stuart clinic, she would not be allowed into the hospital.
Indeed, IPO clients are encouraged to have the birth in the
hospital, and home births are discouraged. Women who sign
up earlier in their pregnancy may later discontinue their
appointments for similar reasons.

The enrollment may be a very passive experience for the
Guatemalan woman in the sense that she may simply follow the
instructions given her by the health workers to sign up for
the program. She may not really understanding what IPO is,
why she must go to another clinic, and often not really
caring because the pregnancy seems to be advancing normally.
Young first time mothers tend to be more "loyal" clients,

rarely missing appointments. However, these women are also WIC clients, and many feel that the tests done during WIC are sufficient, and IPO unnecessary, if not undesireable.

IPO may be considered undesireable on two counts. The first is related to the belief that drawing too much blood is dangerous. At the time of the first check-up three small vials of blood are drawn, but during subsequent check-ups, this is not required. Nonetheless, this practice seems to generate sufficient anxiety so as to discourage the client, especially since the women are not always convinced that this will not be ecessary for subsequent check-ups. The frequent use of ultra-sound tests for determining the size of the fetus and predicting a likely date of birth is also undesireable if the expensive procedure ($150.00) is requested several times by the concerned Health Department midwives.

There are some positive elements of IPO according to the Guatemalan women. If the woman is concerned about some pain, discomfort or other irregularity, she will report it. The health workers are well liked and trusted, and the more tranquil environment of the Health Department in Stuart as compared to WIC in Indiantown is appreciated. Of the procedures during the check-up, the women look forward the most to "listening" to the fetus through a stethescope.

Since three or four women may have an appointment on the same morning, they may all be coordinated by a volunteer to go together, or they may ride the shuttle bus which makes the trip to the Health Department in Stuart once a day on specified days. The advantage of going with a volunteer, besides having a translator, is that a side trip may be made to a super-market, or if all are able, they may stop to get some lunch or even detour to the beach for a picnic. For a young woman who is not working, but spends most of her time in her room, hese outings are especially appreciated and cherished. In addition, the bus schedule is necessarily rigid, and does not allow for such activity.

THE HOSPITAL

A total of thirty-seven Guatemalan children in Indiantown had been born in a hospital in the United States as of the time of this study. Thrity-three were born in Martin Memorial in Stuart, and the others were born in other states. All thirty-seven were born within the past four years, and no one older than four years old was born in a hospital anywhere.

There are, as might be expected, ambivilent attitudes toward the hospital as a place to give birth. Economic constraints often discourage use of the hospital facilities for giving birth. The bill may range from nearly $2,000 for a normal birth, to $4,000 for a birth by Cesarean section. This, combined with prenatal expenses such as ultrasound and ambulance service from Indiantown to Stuart, often makes hospital births prohibitive. Indeed, some Guatemalan families cannot pay their hospital bills at all, which has been to the discredit of those families that do attempt to pay in small monthly installments. The amount of unpaid hospital bills by Guatemalans at one time reached such a high point that the hospital strongly urged the Service Center to work with the Guatemalans to respond to the hospital invoices.

Another cause for concern is the fear of having an undesired operation while in the hospital. In a report to the Florida Catholic Conference to document the incidence of Cesarean section among Guatemalan women (Davey, 1986) it was reported that between October, 1985 and April 1986 there were seventeen hospital births, and 8 home births. Eight of the hospital births were by C-section, two of them with the same woman. Only one woman of the seven, however, understood why the C-section was performed, as was able to communicate it to the interviewer. In another case, the husband was able to explain why the operation was performed. It was clear during the interviews that there was confusion about "the operation", meaning a C-section, and "the operation", meaning a tubal ligation (Davey:1). Thus, some women believed or feared that they had a tubal ligation, when they may actually only have had a C-section. In any event, the apparent lack of understanding, which may partially be a result of reluctance on the part of the women to discuss such a private matter, is no doubt also a result of poor communication between the patient and physician.

In another case, Juana, who had recently given birth in the hospital to her third child expressed that she preferred not to go to the hospital in the event of another pregnancy. Juana was a loyal IPO client even though she had two children in Guatemala only with the help of her mother. The decision to have the hospital birth was made on the belief that is was more modern and, therefore, better. Positive aspects of a hospital birth as expressed by other women include a clean environment, the "goodies" of cans of infant formula, bottles, and disposable diapers, and the presence of a physician and medicines in case of emergency. However, after the birth, Jauna said that the experience was a very lonely one, preferring to have her family close by. The environemnt was not comfortable. She was also concerned that immediately following the birth the nurses had given her a warm sponge bath, and that the child was given a cold bath.

The persistence of home births must be credited primarily to the attitude that pregnancy and birth are normal life events, and that hospitals are usually reserved for emergencies or complications. This is particularly so for women who have previously given with the help of a midwife or friend or on their own. However, although there are at least two Kanjobal midwives in Indiantown, they may not always be available when needed, and some women, especially young mothers-to-be do not feel confident about having a child alone. In this situation, given a choice of having the child at home, possibly alone, or going to the hospital, the latter is preferred. Economic contraints are a close second in considering a hospital birth. Throughout her third pregnancy, Micaela insisted that she did not need to go to IPO nor the hospital, and she scolded her sister for having "wasted" her money when she had her child in the hospital. Unfortunately, Micaela did end up calling the ambulance following the home birth as a result of serious hemorraging.

SUMMARY

The resort to various health resources in Indiantown by Guatemalan refugees as part of an illness episode or for a special program indicates a positive value placed on them.

Most refugees noted that access to clinics and hospitals in Guatemala is more difficult, and that they are glad to have the clinica and the corte so close. The ambulance is also highly valued for emergencies.

The WIC program in the Health Department and the Health Center are the most popular and the most convenient. The fact that all of the most prevalent illnesses in Indiantown perceived by the Guatemalans may be treated in these two facilities supports this. The perceived benefits of both outweigh any hardships incurred in using them, including transportation and loss of a day's wages. Also important, the costs of both are minimal, and both of these facilities have a bilingual receptionist assisting in translation when needed.

For reasons of discreetness the Family Planning program in the Health Center is preferred over the Health Department. This, combined with the availability of male physicians and health workers, instilled a greater sense of confidence in the Health Center, but credibility of the Health Department activities was never questioned. The importance of the presence of a physician, however, is not always a guarantee that treatment will be successful because the patient may believe that an injection is needed and the physician is unlikely to administer one.

Length of residence in Indiantown played a minimal role in the use of the Health Department and Health Center. More single men among the recent arrivals did not know where the clinica or the corte were, and all families were, for the most part, informed soon after arrival. Mandatory immunizations for all school age children, and WIC often account the first experiences with these health facilities for families.

Economic and logistic considerations, combined with less of a perceived need, dampened the use of the hospital for birthing and IPO clinic when it was in Stuart. While the hospital is a respected institution, its credibility in the instance of birthing has been weakened, due primarily to lack of sufficient communication between the patient and the hospital staff. It is important to recognize that economic and transportation constraints will be overcome if use of the hospital is deemed necessary or preferred. Although not specifically addressed during the course of this study and requiring further investigation, it is suggested here that preference for modern medical practices may be correlated with aspirations to be more "modern."

Relying on utilization rates of medical facilities may be misleading as a sole indicator and predictor of health behavior. Although the Guatemalans are indeed going to the various clinics, the question of patient compliance with

"doctor's orders" is left unanswered. Some of these are
related to a misunderstanding of the goals of the health
programs. Curative services, for example, are more
important than preventive programs such as WIC and IPO.
Indeed, certain aspects of these preventive programs may be
interpreted as health-threatening, such as the excessive
drawing of blood, or the recommendation to include in the
diet cheese and other dairy products that may disagree with
a lactose intolerant individual. There is also more concern
with therapeutic techniques, such as the use of pills in
lieu of injections. This is essentially a communication and
education problem and suggests that optimum use of such
health care resources has yet to be achieved.

In all cases, there was a considerable dependence on
the availability of a Service Center volunteer to inform the
Guatemalans of various health services, to provide
transportation and translation services, to the point of the
volunteer coordinating appointments and then reminding women
of them. Often, the volunteer would act as an advisor and
intermediary as well as translator. There is little doubt
that without this assistance, utilization of these health
resources would have been reduced.

This chapter attempted to point out some important
factors influencing perceptions and use of health programs.
However, for the demonstration of the link between

knowledge, percpetions, beliefs and behavior, an in-depth
study of the decision process involved in purposive action
is required, and beyond the scope of this preliminary
investigation. Evenso, four major criteria that must be
considered in this process have been discovered: the
perceived seriousness of the illness; previous experience
with a particular illness and remedy; previous experience
with a particular medical facility; accessibility of the
medical facility, which can either be accessible in terms of
available resources and transportation, or not.

CHAPTER FIVE
DISCUSSION: KANJOBAL HEALTH IN INDIANTOWN

This chapter discusses the results of the study of the health behavior of the Guatemalan refugees in Indiantown. The Kanjobal people have become part of the health and illness reality that characterizes much of the rural migrant work force of the United States. In particular, this includes various diseases endemic to rural Florida, poor nutrition, and the socio-economic conditions that promote them, primarily poverty and high rates of mobility. A similar situation has been described for much of Guatemala in its recent history as well (Appendix C).

The Mayan refugees in Indiantown have brought with them their unique cultural knowledge, beliefs, values, attitudes and perceptions resulting from their historical experiences with health and illness both as individuals and as a cultural group. These factors necessarily set them apart from other groups in Indiantown. A cultural perspective on health behavior takes into account these factors in the incidence of illness and differential use of available health resources. Tapping this kind of information may be useful to health workers and other community workers as they strive to help the population they serve.

126

THE NATURE OF ILLNESS

The Guatemalans have not come to Indiantown as "empty vessels," devoid of any knowledge, beliefs and perceptions of health and illness. Traditional Mayan epistemology in Guatemala has as its core several beliefs regarding the causes of illness and other misfortunes which both support and serve as a rationale for traditional health maintenance and curing practices.

Modern biomedical practices in Guatemala have introduced effective cures for diseases as well as preventive measures, such as immunizations. In Guatemala these modern medicines were respected and valued. For the most part, the refugees consider themselves to be healthier in Indiantown than in Guatemala, although there is not as great a value placed on oral medications. The threat of sickness, of losing one's ability to work, remains an important variable in adopting the sick role. Prevention, especially in a threatening environment, therefore, plays a major role in everyday activities.

The refugees identified various illnesses they perceive to be most prevalent and problematic in Indiatown. Two of these, diarrhea and fever, are those considered to be most prevalent and problematic to both the refugees and the Health Center. Health seeking behavior may be viewed as a process involving stages beginning with symptom recognition and ending with symptom relief. Only those illnesses classified as "new" or novel are not accounted for by an existing "logic" that explains not only what causes some malaise, but also how to prevent and cure them.

Illnesses are often presented in the form of symptoms. For example, diarrhea, rather than being a symptom of a disorder of the digestive tract, is an illness resulting from a particular state of humoral imbalance. Similarly, calentura, described as fever, is an illness with its own etiology. Thus, treatment may seem to take the form of "symptomology," for example to cool down a hot fever with a cool drink, or to warm up a head cold caused by cold night air with a hot drink. Over-the-counter remedies such as analgesics and temporary (symptomatic) relief from coughs and fever are also considered useful. The potential health danger lies in the belief that if the symptoms no longer persist, the person must be cured, and that, consequently, the underlying (biological) causes of the illness will not be checked in a timely fashion.

A POUND OF PREVENTION, AN OUNCE OF CURE

Appropriate actions and behavior for the prevention of illness depends on an understanding of the nature of illness

etiology. The perceptions of the causes of illnesses and
their cures may be be viewed as reflecting the environmental
conditions being experienced, and successful adaptive
responses to these conditions. Given an epistemology that
includes humoral pathologies, for example, the prescibed
preventive behavior in the threat of possible "over-heating"
may include drinking "cooling" sodas, but also avoiding
excessive cooling. It is not so surprising, therefore, to
note that the Kanjobal Mayans, coming from the cool
Cuchumatan highlands, are concerned in the subtropical
Florida flatlands with sicknesses that appear to be caused
by conditions of extreme heat or cold. There is a constant
vigilence so as not to upset the delicate humoral balance
that signifies a state of well-being.

     In addition to the belief in the hot-cold theory of
disease causation, contagion is also recognized as a source
of sickness. This is primarily through tactile means, such
as touching the clothes of an "infected" person, or by
introducing a foreign object into the body, like worms.
Other notions of contagion based on the germ theory of
disease, however, were not evident. Thus, a multi-purpose
rag used to wipe a runny nose may also be used to wipe an
infant feeding bottle, a dirty hand, and more.

     The health resources most widely utilized and highly
valued by the refugees are primarily curative in

orientation, with the exception of the WIC program. The
primary motive is to receive medication, while a medical
diagnosis is sought in the event of an unfamiliar illness or
in the case of doubt as to the actual cause. The Health
Center treats many Guatemalans with complaints of diarrhea,
upset stomache, _calentura_ and _catarro_. Resort to the
clinica often follows unsuccessful self-treatments with over
the counter remedies, and despite possible economic or
logistics constraints, medical consultation will be sought
if the need is perceived.

The Kanjobal midwives are actively involved with
assisting and consulting many pregnant or would be pregnant
refugee women. The _promotor de salud_ is also sought out for
advice as well as an occasional request to administer
curative medications (although the request will be turned
down by the _promotor_). In both cases, these health
caretakers do not discourage their clients from seeking
professional medical help either at the clinic or the
hospital.

Preventive health programs like WIC and IPO attract
clients for a variety of reasons which may include the
checks for the purchase of needed food, the opportunity for
an informal social gathering, and curiosity about lab
results. Some families may not use these resources because
there is no felt need.

MAYANS AND PATIENT SATISFACTION

    Results of this study suggest that the Guatemalans in
Indiantown are, for the most part, satisfied with the health
care available to them.   Improved health status, as
perceived by the refugees, however, is not due to the
quality of disease specific treatments and medical
procedures so much as to improved living conditions: for
many this means nothing more than enough food to eat, and a
roof over their heads. Like the Hmong refugees in Nebraska,
health is not considered a major problem   (Meredith and
Cramer, 1982:355-357).   Instead, finding that safe refuge,
housing, and suitable employment are the top priorities
while adjusting to refugee life in the United States.   Only
insofar as illness interferes with one's ability to work,
for example the ability to pick the maximum number of crates
in a day, is the state of one's health of primary concern.

    Satisfaction with Indiantown health resources, it must
be noted, has been described in terms of the favorable
comparison with Guatemalan medical facilities and personnel.
Only certain Guatemalan medications appear to have an edge
over those in Indiantown. One must ask, therefore, what is
the extent of this satisfaction, what are the criteria, and
how is this reflected in health-seeking behavior?   In what
ways has satisfaction been influenced by previous positive

or negative experiences with modern medicine or traditional curing systems? How is this reflected in behavior?

An examination of the social and cultural context of modern health care in Guatemala provide some insight into the probable nature of previous experiences with modern medicine. Those areas of Latin America characterized by a large indigenous population have often been described as having two disctinct, but not mutually exclusive, cultures (Beals, 1953:329). In Guatemala, although a numerical majority, those of Indian descent have continued to represent a political and economic minority, a legacy of Guatemala's colonial heritage (Stein and Stein, 1970).

Many Mayan groups have been able to maintain their indigenous identity, their native dress and language, throughout the centuries, primarily as a result of the development of peasant closed corporate communities, actually fostered by the Spanish Crown as a controlling device to check colonists' and indigenous power (Wolf, 1959:214). Those most likely to be in positions of authority have been ladinos, or persons of hispanic cultural heritage, and often only Spanish speaking.

Today, any formal or bureaucratic affairs relating to the greater "national culture" undertaken by an indigenous person, such as dealing with civil authorities or medical personnel, may still be viewed as a cross-cultural experience. The most recent violent and often brutal actions against Indian peasants represent an attempt at breaking this bastion of traditionalism and "backwardness." Such "modernizing" national policies prompted the massive movements of involuntary and voluntary migrants and refugees

In seeking refuge in the United States, the Guatemalans found themselves still a powerless minority but in relation to a different culture, still struggling for survival. The men, with greater Spanish speaking skills than the women, continued to take on tasks requiring dealing with authorities of this new dominant culture, including finding housing and negotiating rent, finding a job, getting a post office box, going to the health center or health department, and enrolling the children in school. Often, this also requires a bilingual intermediary. Fortunately, many of the schools' personnel, the receptionists at the Health Department and Health Center, and the Service Center volunteers were, at the time of this study, bilingual in Spanish. Women, having only a minimal of Spanish skills, are once again in an environment in which the dominant language spoken is not their own. In addition, several Guatemalan children have been able to translate from English for their parents.

Given the refugees' previous experiences with ladinos in positions of authority, one may wonder whether similar behavior patterns of relating to authorities, such as health workers, persist in Indiantown. For example, the Guatemalans described the American doctors and nurses and medications as being the same as in Guatemala. It is suggested here that, due to the common characteristics of modern, Western medical practice in terms of the rituals involved in physcian-patient relations and in and the familiar "tools of the trade" (a white lab jacket, the thermometer, the blood pressure monitor, etc.), the refugees expected that the medical personnel in Indiantown and the hospital would behave in a manner similar to that of the ladino doctors in Guatemala.

A cursory examination of a situation described by Woods (1970) of the introduction of modern medical practices in the Guatemalan town of San Lucas Toliman is instructive. The new doctor, who maintained his more important social ties and a separate residence in Guatemala City, is presented in sharp contrast to the close personal and social involvement of the traditional curers with their patients. In the medical facility, the Indian patients had to register with a ladino teenager and then wait on a first-come, first-serve basis in a crowded waiting area. The ladino medical personnel conducted interviews with their clients in an impersonal and business-like manner, with few questions asked about symptoms, eating habits and body functions.

Ignorant, if not distainful of the Indian culture, the doctor did not allude to any of the behavioral irregularities which the Indians in San Lucas believed led to many illnesses. After the examination, a patient would be turned over to a nurse to administer the required treatment, instructions, medications or prescriptions. Diagnosis, when offered, was generally couched in unfamiliar scientific terminology such that patient would leave with little knowledge of his ailment or its cause.

With few exceptions, this situation describes the health care system in the United States. The doctor's waiting room in San Lucas was always full because the Mayans were well aware of the obvious benefits of modern medicines for the cure of certain diseases. The primary focus of patient satisfaction in this case was the efficacy of the medication, and not whether or not the physician demonstrated the appropriate "bedside manner" that might be expected of a traditional curer. Similar observations were made from recent arrivals in Indiantown as well as those who have resided in Indiantown for longer periods. Thus, from this perspective it is not surprising that the Guatemalans expressed satisfaction with the medical serivces received in Indiantown. Satisfaction with health care received is due, at least in part, to the fact that their expectations were indeed met.

THE COMMUNITY AND PUBLIC HEALTH

Although the Guatemalan refugees do not constitute a homogenous group free from internal conflict and stress, they all share common health problems. These include not only the illnesses themselves, but the conditions that provoke them. They also share common beliefs and perceptions as to the incidence of certain illness, their causes, and appropriate therapeutic responses. Furthermore, they share similar experiences in meeting their health needs in this new environment and culture.

It is clear that with the assistance of the "helping community", primarily the Service Center, the Guatemalans are quickly adapting to their new situation. The Service Center has been the hub of activity for organizing transportation, translation, and providing educational services for literacy, developing English skills, and pre-natal classes. The Service Center is the first to be contacted by Indiantown health workers in questions regarding the Guatemalan population. In many ways, the Service Center has been recognized as "responsible" for the refugees by both health workers and the refugees themselves.

Unfortunately, this caretaker role that has been assigned to the Service Center has proven more deterimental than helpful not only to the organization but also to the people they serve. Increasing time and energies devoted to providing services for the Guatemalans such as transportation and translation, have resulted in a kind of dependency on the Service Center with expectations that it will continue to provide these services. Indeed, their convenience has been a major incentive for the participation of families in certain health programs, primarily WIC and IPO. By the end of the period of this investigation, however, the Service Center had adopted a policy of providing transportation only in unusual or emergency situations.

Many of the illnesses and health care experiences of the Guatemalans in Indiantown are also shared by a great proportion of the non-Guatemalan residents of Indiantown. Those most readily recognized among them include language barriers, low levels of formal education, poverty and lack of transportation. People may not so easily realize, however, that they share the same illnesses or even what these may be. Problems related to poor housing, overcrowding, inadequate sanitation facilities, and garbage disposal as well as violence, drug and alcohol abuse affect the entire community, which, by virtue of their residence, includes the Guatemalans. In a very real sense, these are all public health issues requiring community participation for their solution.

REFUGEE AND IMMIGRANT HEALTH

This study demonstrates that, in many ways, the characteristics of this refugee group are not so different from those of other immigrants. Holt (1981) suggests that some degree of community solidarity will result because refugees will be "naturally" encouraged to find their primary security among their own members. Indeed, the extensive network that connects San Miguel Acatan with Indiantown and places in between and the large number of refugees in Indiantown related to each other support this observation.

By definition, however, refugees are unlike other migrant and immigrant groups in that they are forced to leave their homes, possessions and jobs. The social disruption associated with some of the precipitating factors of refugee situations may have serious consequences on the family and the "new" community structure. Kinship networks as that described above, and economic ties that at one time may have contributed to the home community identity and organization are likely to be broken during migration (Chambers, 1982). In the Indiantown case these networks seem to have been exaggerated.

Conflict may result among refugees along with social disintegration if social ranking at home depended on

relative wealth or on differing lifestyles, or with changes
in housing patterns which force different groups to live in
close proximity.   Also, particularly in the case of
political refugees, it cannot be assumed that even if the
immediate problems leading to becoming a refugee may be
shared, the underlining reasons may not. For example, the
Kanjobal people all fled the violence in their country, but
they may either identify with the Government forces or the
guerillas, depending on their experiences.

Social breakdown among refugees may also be fostered by
economic damage. Loss of land, lifestock, or other form of
livelihood and its repercussions and cultural adaptations
that may be required in a new environment may have direct
implications for refugee health.   "Forced idleness" and
overcrowding of Guatemalans in Mexican refugee camps has
been identified as the root cause of intergenerational
conflict and the large numbers of extra-marital births
(Durand, 1984:10).   Similarly, a study of Afghan Pushtun
refugees in Pakistan reports a high incidence of what has
been identified as "dependency syndrom," a psychological
malaise associated with psychosomatic symptoms, including
various aches, coughs, unidentifiable fevers, hyperacidity
and digestive disorders (York and Grant, 1980).

Like the Guatemalans, the Pushtun are considered
particularly affected because agriculture and other

land-based pursuits that are culturally important are for
the most part not permitted them as refugees. In this
sense, one can appreciate that inspite of the current living
conditions of the refugees in Indiantown, this may indeed be
the preferred option.

SUMMARY

     When life is characterized as a daily struggle for
survival, health and illness take on different meanings from
those who enjoy a more prosperous if not stable life. For
many, health may simply mean a state of being able to carry
out one's responsibilities, and not the absence of disease.
For refugees, immigrants and other migrants there are
generally many difficulties in obtaining adequate health
care, especially in the rural setting. In addition,
problems accessing adequate care are often compounded by
cultural differences such as language, beliefs, and
expectations due to previous experiences. All together,
these are some of the factors which influence health
behavior.

CHAPTER SIX
RECOMMENDATIONS

As an applied project, one of the goals of this study
as stated in the introductory chapter is to go beyond the
discovery, description and explanation of health seeking
behavior. This goal was to be able to take the information
and formulate some recommendations for problem solving
action. This chapter presents some recommendations for the
Indiantown health workers and the service community.

There is no doubt among any of Indiantown residents of
the patience and good will of their local health workers.
Their continued efforts and concern to improve health care
delivery are commended by all. One must not assume, howver,
that although the Guatemalans in Indiantown express overall
satisfaction with the health resources available, low
expectations are not justified nor does it preclude the
possibility of improving health care delivery. Central to
this, and clear to all concerned, is the problem of
communication between the health workers and their Kanjobal
clients. Communication, in this sense, extends beyond the
ability to translate words, but also to communicate
concepts. Given the nature of some of the health problems
of Indiantown, however, health must also be considered more
than a matter of individual concern.

141

COMMUNICATION AND EDUCATION

Communication is necessarily a two-way road in which a
message must not only be sent but also received. In the
case in which a translator is required, the situation may
arise of the creation of a kind of "toll-booth" in which the
price paid is some potentially vital information that may
"miss the off-ramp." When two translators were needed, as
was the case with only Kanjobal speaking refugees, the
problem was only compounded. In much the same way that a
social scientist may in some cases need to rely on the
ability of a translator to perform his duties accurately, he
must be aware that consciously or unconsciously, the
translator is filtering the questions and information,
presenting what he deems important and in the manner he
feels most appropriate. This was an inevitable occurence as
I found out working as a translator for the Guatemalans.

The problem is not just one of lack of language skills.
Kanjobal children becoming increasingly fluent in English
are not able to effectively translate the biomedical style
of symptom description and diagnosis into the "folk" style.
Much of the epistemology of these different models not only
defies their translation skills, but also the extent of
their own knowledge and understanding of the biomedical
aspects of health and illness.   Thus,   a   concerned

nutritionist must wonder not only if a translation of the message that leafy greens and red meats have a high iron content is complete, but also whether the entire message was understood by the client. A physician must rely on the accuracy of the translator for the description and history of his client's symptoms.

Another awkward situation may be illustrated by a case in which a young Kanjobal boy with some English skills was asked to translate for a couple unrelated to him seeking family planning. Not only was the subject considered inappropriate for the boy by the values of his culture, but the extent of his own understanding of reproduction limited his translating ability. In addition, the boy and the couple involved recall the session with deep embarassment. One may then appreciate that this is really a double-edged problem of communication and education.

1. Community Level Health Workers: One unique approach to a similar problem in providing health care assistance to a Navajo tribe has been documented by Adair and Deuschle (1970). In this case, the socio-cultural, economic, geographic and medical problems seen on the reservation in 1955 were similar to the health conditions in many underdeveloped countries. A joint decision made by the United States Public Health Service, Indian Health Services, and the Navajo tribal government to improve the Navajo

health care system resulted in the Many Farms project, developed by a research team from Cornell. The assumption of the project was that cultural gaps could be mitigated, and that and in-depth knowledge of the cultural and language differences can help the health professionals strengthen the overall health service program.

The communication barriers between the Navajo and health workers was attacked from two sides. First, bilingual Navajo men and women were trained to the level of field nurse assistant. They were given extensive education and training in medical interpretation, through the team efforts of a Navajo nurse and linguistic experts, with frequent monitoring of ongoing medical interpretation problems. Secondly, the non-Navajo health professionals improved their communication skills by learning about Navajo culture, customs and beliefs.

Indiantown may benefit greatly from a program to develop similar community level health workers among the Guatemalans. Indeed, it is tempting to recruit the already trained promotor de salud to fill this position in some offical capacity and has been utilized in other refugee situations (Simmonds, 1983; Cutts, 1984). It must be remembered, however, that the promotor was trained by Catholic missionaries in the particular method of the "Dio es Sano" diocese, and continues to be active in Catholic

Youth Group activities in Indiantown. His strong association with the Church may alienate him from the Protestant groups in town.

Training the midwives may also be considered, but their level of formal education is minimal at best, and language skills to be learned should include both Spanish and English. One other major drawback to the use of community level health workers is the risk of breach of confidentiality and privacy, especially in the case of the medicalization of social health problems.

This approach may be very attractive to a health care system striving to generate increased community participation and active involvement in local health care issues. This is especially so if an already heavily burdened public health department is able to utilize the research resources of a university to help develop such a program. However, there are other lessons to be learned from the Many Farms project. Among these are the need to insure continued economic and managerial support, and the importance of maintaining a balance of professional health providers and community health worker support appropriate for acceptable high quality care at the Health Center and Health Department. In addition, the initial heavy investments in time and human resources may prove overwhelming.

In this case, a more realistic starting point may be a temporary or limited use of those persons already knowledgeable about health problems among the Guatemalans. The health workers may find it very helpful to seek out the advice or temporary assistance of the midwives or promotores and other community leaders. Establishing a rapport between these various health resources may facilitate the implementation of public health projects such as mass immunizations for adults as well as children, and tuberculosis screenings, because of their knowledge of how best to approach such a project. By promoting an equalitarian relationship between professional health workers and these Guatemalans, any conflict over patient control, mutual caretaker respect (Scrimshaw and Burleigh, 1978) may be avoided.

2. Developing Communication Skills: Health workers may also strive to improve their communication skills, even if they must rely on a translator. Perhaps the time in which these skills are most useful is during the initial interview with a client presenting a complaint.

In one strategy, rather than asking if one's kidneys are hurting, the question may be accompanied with a gesture indicating the kidney area. Encouraging the patient to indicate where symptoms are felt without having to give it a "proper name" may alleviate language barriers by simply not requiring the use of words that may not be necessary.

The doctor or nurse must be careful not to assume that the patient or the translator understand the questions being asked. For example, specific questions should be asked about the symptoms presented, including asking the patient for his or her own diagnosis. This may provide the doctor with further clues as to what ails the person.

In one case, for example, a woman with limited knowledge of Spanish complained of stomach cramps and pain accompanied by bleeding. The physician, understandably concerned about such symptoms asked from where she was bleeding. Her description was confused if not uncertain, suggesting that she was bleeding from both the rectum and the vagina. Concerned that she may have either an ulcer or an ovarian cyst or both, she was sent off to have various tests. However, had the doctor questioned her a bit more carefully about her own diagnosis during the initial interview, he would have found that she was menstruating at the time and that she had suspected worms. Only after a series of expensive and time consuming exams provided negative results was a stool sample taken. This exam was positive for two kinds of helminths.

3. WIC Instructional Materials: Research indicates that folk beliefs may change with the empirical knowledge

gained through practical experience (Erasmus, 1952) but knowledge of nutrition does not necessarily imply that behavior will be affected. Although many WIC clients are able to recite the nutritionists' recommendations, the meanings are often misconstrued or misunderstood. Indeed, the women participating in WIC often do not understand the point of the nutrition classes. Part of this is due to the language barrier. Even if the class is given in Spanish by a translator or pre-recorded, is difficult to follow, and unfamiliar terms and concepts are frequently used.

One solution may be to translate the materials into Kanjobal. In the event of the lack of a translator knowledgeable in both languages of the concepts involved, inaccuarate or otherwise inappropriate materials may result.

An alternative approach to material presentation may take into account the cultural pattern of describing illnesses as symptoms. Classes organized around the topics of dietary iron, calcium, or other nutrients, may be "turned around" so that the topics focus on specific symptoms of health and illness, and foods that can promote good health. These need not be translated in Kanjobal, but should at least be presented Spanish with a minimum of technical terminology.

For example, a class could be organized around the topic of weak or low blood, its symptoms, how to prevent it and how to alleviate it by proper diet. Another class may focus on growth, and so on. Women may also be encouraged to share their own knowledge of these "illnesses." Cause of the illness, as per the biomedical model, need not even be introduced at this point.

One interesting WIC class that was well received by the Kanjobal women was given by a Service Center volunteer with nursing training and experience in Guatemala. The topic was calcium. The point that was immediately picked up by the women was that, even though they may not have been aware, in Guatemala calcium was made available in the diet by virtue of the lime-soaked maize used to make tortillas.

The volunteer told the women that although they had calcium in their traditional diets, because their food habits were changing they had to find other ways of providing their bodies with these nutrients. Other sources of calcium that were available in WIC foods included milk and cheese. The comparison of foods and food habits from Guatemala with those in Indiantown was interesting to the women and provided an excellent common ground on which to base further discussion.

4.   Program Goals: Perhaps more fundamentally, however, programs goals of both WIC and IPO should be well articulated when the client signs up for the programs, and at critical times, such as recertification and when

"graduating" a client. This is only to protect the
integrity of the programs as preventive programs, especially
for unborn children and borderline nutritional risk cases,
and curative for those already at risk.

COMMUNITY HEALTH

> To date, the [Community Development]
> experience has had little impact on the
> planning and operations of [Primary
> Health Care] programs which, I believe,
> can profit significantly from the
> lessons from [Community Development]
> (Foster, 1982: 184)

The sine qua non of community health is the quality of
the relationship between health providers and the population
they serve. Central to this is communication. However, in
broader terms of community development, health implies that
level of wholeness and well-being when people are able to
work together effectively to meet their needs in a
responsible and self-reliant manner. It follows from this
that a precondition to being a fully "healthy" person is a
clear understanding of oneself in relation to other people,
as well as to the factors that influence one's well-being.
Therefore, those activities that help to develop a critical
awareness should form a vital part of any health program.

       1. Self-Reliance: The Service Center must be
appreciated as an invaluable resource for the health

workers. Due to the intimate relationships developed with many Guatemalans with Service Center personnel, they are able to provide an additional insight into the Guatemalans' lifestyles and other factors that affect their health. Most of the health workers do not live in Indiantown and altough working in town, are isolated from the reality the daily lives of their clients, often not aware of critical events in community. All interaction takes place within clinic walls, and does not extend into the community.

The apparent dependence on the Service Center volunteer activities for taking the initiative and responsibility for the health care of the Guatemalans has been noted. However, since the recent relocation of the IPO clinic from Stuart to Indiantown, and with the new transportation policy at the Center, refugee women are no longer requiring nor requesting transportation with as much frequency. Some Guatemalans have even organized among themselves for occassional transportation to Stuart and West Palm Beach for shopping. In addition, the Kanjobales do not avoid going to the health facilities if they feel they must. It is suggested that the Service Center continue to encourage the refugees to develop self-reliant means as part of a greater community development program.

2. Informing the Community: The Service Center has also had a definite role in the dissemination of information

on health resources in Indiantown. This could be expanded
to include "the bigger picture." For example, many
Guatemalans are not aware of a national migrant health care
system, and many assume that the WIC program either does not
exist elsewhere or is non-transferable. The Service Center
has also been key to assiting refugees to file for political
asylum. This should also include informing the Guatemalan's
of their rights as refugees and migrants with respect to
various social services.

Encouraging community health awareness in the local
schools is another channel to pursue. All children,
Guatemalans and others, may be introduced to basic
traditional preventive care measures, such as good nutrition
and dental hygiene, which may be accompanied by field trips
to the Health Center and the Health Department to learn
about these vital health resources in their community.
Regular units addressing local halth issues may be included
as part of the school curricula. Specific age or grade
groups may be targeted. Such an effort may be coordinated
by the Health Department and the schools or by concerned
parents and teachers willing to work together for this.

3. A Functional Approach: If indeed the Guatemalan
population shares common health problems, this may provide a
common base for community development efforts. Community
health issues could be addressed by health workers within

the context of various activities that would bring the
questions and issues out of the clinic and "into the field."
These may include environmental and preventive health issues
specific to agricultural workers.

In 1985, as part of the activities of the first annual
"Fiesta de San Miguel" commemorating the patron saint of the
town from where most of the refugees come, the Health
Department was asked by the Service Center, the sponsoring
agent, to participate. Reactions from Guatemalan mothers to
a well-baby contest held by the Indiantown Health Department
nurses were enthusiastic. This represented a novel
interaction between health workers and the community outside
of the clinic walls in a festive environment. This gave the
health workers a high profile among not only those clients
with whom they have worked but also among those they have
not.

However, it must be emphasized that presence of the
health workers should not pose a threat to client-health
worker confidentiality. Such activities should be limited
to addressing community-wide problems.

4. Documenting Volunteer Experiences: The Service
Center invites new volunteers to come and work in Indiantown
on a one year basis. This attracts people from all over the
nation for a variety of reasons. Most volunteers have very
little or no experience in community development programs

and few have any professional training. In the course of
one year of hard work, however, they come to learn many
things about how to develop and carry out projects, and,
primarily, how to work with the people they help.

Unfortunately, to date no volunteer has kept any
records of his or her activities, of efforts that were
fruitful and those not so successful. With the rapid and
high turn-over of volunteers, the benefit of having a
history on hand may avoid the repeating of past errors and
saving much "start-up" time. An archive documenting these
past experiences can help orient new volunteers and to
insure the succesfull continuation of existing projects. It
may also provide information about other projects that did
not last and why.

Creating such an archive may be very simple. The
volunteers may record progress on a regular weekly or
monthly basis, or as appropriate. Included would be the
projects they work on, noting key information such as
materials needed, time spent, valuable contacts,
descriptions of positive and negative events, and
projections for future needs. These logs may be kept in a
binder in the Service Center library for easy access. Prior
to ending the one year term, a summary of experiences and
recommendations should be presented to the Center.

5. <u>The Need for a Greater Understanding</u>: Perhaps the most important recommendation to be offered is the need for continued efforts to promote a greater understanding of the plight of not only the Kanjobal refugees in Indiantown, but of other refugee situations throughout the world.

Research needs include a study of decision-making in the face of illness, and factors relating to emotional and physiological stress, as well as changing perspectives and medical orientation through time. Obviously, the quality and usefulness of future work could only benefit several-fold with the knowledge of the Guatemalans' native language.

From the perspective of the the applied social scientist, it is hoped that the results from such investigations may contribute to our understanding of the broader problems of refugees, refugee health care and approaches to their solutions. As concerned citizens, it must not be forgotten that there is almost invariably a political cause for people to become refugees, and ultimately the solutions to many of these problems require political decisions. The health of refugees maybe directly affected by these decisions. As some authors soberly note:

> There may be political forces which
> prevent information from being obtained

> or services from being optimally
> directed. Furthermore, health workers
> may be confronted by violations of human
> rights, which they cannot afford to
> ignore anymore than they could consider
> neglecting the absence of other basic
> necessities such as food, water and
> shelter (Dick and Simmonds, 1983:198).

Therefore, the causes of illness and death among refugee
groups throughout the world and the provision of health care
cannot be viewed apart from the context which gave rise to
the refugee situation in the first place. It is, in a very
tragic sense, a matter of life and death.

A HOPE FOR THE FUTURE

When the refugees fled their homes in Guatemala they
sought not only a more secure present, but came to the
United States with aspirations for a better future. Despite
the physical and emotional trauma suffered by the Mayans as
victims of national violence in Guatemala and as refugees,
it is clear that their courage and determination to survive
persevere. The current lack of official government support
for their plight has denied them access to various refugee
assistance programs, and leaves them open to the abuses
received by all undocumented laborers in the United States.

It is difficult to encourage community action when
individual survival is a struggle. By the same token,
however, community action may be required for survival, and

more, an improved quality of life in general. It is indeed a fortunate twist of fate that these Mayan refugees found their refuge in Indiantown, a town well equipped with an active helping community, and a population accustomed to receiving peoples of diverse backgrounds.

There is little doubt that these people will not only continue to survive, but will indeed strive for that better life. A look to the future suggests that like other immigrant groups, people will continue to adjust to their new social, cultural and economic environment. Many refugee children already are trilingual, and 1986 marks the year that the first Kanjobal, a woman, graduates with a Associate of Arts degree from a local community college. As opportunities for survival, better jobs, and housing appear, there is no doubt that the refugees will also continue to disperse, but the networks that have kept people together between places in Guatemala, Mexico, Los Angeles, Arizona, and Florida remain strong.

APPENDIX A
CENSUS FORM

Address: Total no. of residents:
                                   No. relatives:

Head of Family:
   Age:
   Birthplace:
   Understands Spanish: Good Some None (subjective)
   Speaks Spanish: G   S   N   (subjective)
   Reads: G   S   N
   Years of schooling:

Spouse:
   Age:
   Birthplace:
   Understands Spanish: G   S   N   (subjective)
   Speaks Spanish: G   S   N   (subjective)
   Reads: G   S   N
   Years of schooling:

No. of children in U.S.:   Guatemala: Elsewhere?:

Name of Child / date of birth / birthplace / school?/
employed?
1.
2.
3.
4.
5.
6.
7.

When did father leave Guatemala?
When did mother leave?   Children?

When did father arrive in Indiantown?
When did mother arrive?   Children?

Did you spend any time elsewhere before coming to Indiantown?
Where?

What kind of work did father do in Guatemala?
What kind of work did mother do in Guatemala?

158

Are you presently employed? father: Y   N   What do you do?
                            mother: Y   N   What do you do?

Has anyone in the family been sick in the last year?   Y   N
    Who?
    What happened?

    What did you do?

If there are children less than five years, or if mother is
pregnant, do you receive WIC checks?
    How long (mos.) have you been receiving WIC checks?
    Who told you about the checks? Friend   SC Volunteer
Spouse   Other

Has anyone visited the "clinica", hospital or a doctor
here? Y N
    If Yes, where: Why?
    What was the treatment?
    Are you cured now?
    What do you think about the (clinica, hospital, etc.)?
        (do you know where they are?)

Did you ever go to a clinic, hospital or a doctor in
Guatemala or Mexico? Y   N
    If Yes, where: Why?
    What was the treatment?
    Are you cured now?
    What do you think about that (clinic, hospital, etc.)?

What is your religion? Father: Catholic   Adventist
Other   Nothing
                        Mother: C   A   O   N

Do you own a car?

Who does the shopping?
    How often do you do the shopping?
    Where is the shopping done?   Why?
    How much do you spend on food/wk?

Why did you leave Guatemala?

Have you filed for political asylum?   Y   N

APPENDIX B
BOOKER PARK BLOCK SURVEY

	1984	1986	
Total lots surveyed	462	462	--
Total buildings surveyed	330	333	+.9%
Condition of buildings*			
good	126	139	+9.4%
fair	111	121	+8.3%
poor	62	36	-26%
Septic system problems	100	94	-6%
Garbage	53	72	+26%
Privy	6	2	-40%
Farm Animals	37	22	-15%
Mosquito breeding areas	26	16	-38%
Rodent harborage	NA	112	--
Raw sewage	43	NA	--

Other public health problems:
  flies, broken plumbing,
  illegal septic system,
  broken tank lids,
  rats, etc.   120   NA   --

*   Good condition - no evident deterioration, sound
                     construction.
    Fair condition - mild to moderate exterior deterioration.
    Poor condition - unit delapidated, unsound.

CASES OF ENTERICS

	Indiantown (~7% of population)	Rest of Martin County (~93% of population)
Rotavirus	28	72
Salmonellas	40	60
Shigella	100	0
Giardia	90	10
Hookworm	75	25
Trichuris	100	0
Entamoeba coli	100	0
Entamoeba nana	100	0
Entamoeba hartmanni	100	0
Food poisoning	20	80
I. Butschelli	100	0
Tapeworm	100	0

Source: Martin County Commissioner, Stuart, Florida

160

APPENDIX C
INDICATORS RELATED TO LIFE EXPECTANCY

Life Expectancy, Infant and Child Mortality for Guatemala,
Mexico and the United States, 1960, 1980.

	Life expectancy @ birth (yrs.)		Infant mortality rate (0-1 yrs.)		Child death (1-4 yrs.)	
	1960	1980	1960	1980	1960	1980
Guatemala	47	59	92	70	10	6
Mexico	58	65	91	56	10	4
United States	70	74	26	13	1	1

Daily per Capita Calorie Supply of Guatemala, Mexico and the
United States, 1977, 1981.

	Total		As % of Req't.	
	1977	1981	1977	1981
Guatemala	2,156	2,045	92	93
Mexico	2,654	2,905	113	121
United States	3,484	3,647	127	138

Populations per Physician in Guatemala, Mexico and United
States, 1960, 1970 and 1980.

	1960	1970	1980
Guatemala	4,420	2,560	8,610
Mexico	1,820	1,260	...
United States	750	580	520

Source: World Bank Development Report, 1982, Tables 21, 22;
World Bank Development Report, 1984, Tables 23, 24.

161

Rural (Republic - Dept. of Guatemala) crude birth, death and natural increase rates, by ethnic group differences, 1950- 1973

	1950-54	1955-59	1960-64	1965-69	1970-73
Mayan Indian					
Birth	51.1	51.5	47.7	45.2	44.9
Death	24.5	24.5	20.3	14.8	30.1
Natural increase	26.6	27.0	27.4	25.2	30.1
Years to double	26.1	25.7	25.3	27.5	23.1
Ladino					
Birth	51.6	48.6	48.9	45.6	44.9
Death	17.2	15.7	13.5	15.5	13.6
Natural increase	34.4	32.9	35.4	30.1	31.3
Years to double	20.1	21.1	19.6	23.1	22.2
Differences (Indian - Ladino)					
Birth	-0.5	2.9	-1.2	-0.4	0.0
Death	7.3	8.8	6.8	4.5	1.2
Natural increase	-7.8	-5.9	-8.0	-4.9	-1.2

Source: Early: 1982

REFERENCES

Adair, John and Kurt W. Deuschle
    1970   The People's Health: Medicine and Anthropology in
            a Navajo Community. New York: Meredith
            Corporation.

Adams, Richard and A. J. Rubel
    1967   "Sickness and Social Relations." In, Maning Nash,
            ed., The Handbook of Middle American Indians, Vol.
            6, pp. 333-356. Austin: University of Texas
            Press.

Applebaum, Richard P.
    1967   "San Idelfonso Ixtahuacan, Guatemala: Un Estudio
            Sobre la Migracion Temporal, Sus Causas y
            Consequencias." Cuadernos del Seminario de
            Integracion Social de Guatemala. Primera Serie,
            No. 17.

Ashabranner, Brent
    1986   Children of the Maya: A Guatemalan Indian Odyssey.
            New York: Dodd, Mead and Company.

Beals, Ralph
    1953   "Social Stratification in Latin America." American
            Journal of Sociology 68:54-69.

Browning, R. H. and T. J. Northcutt
    1961   On the Season. Florida State Board of Health,
            Monograph Number 2.

Castillo, Manuel Angel
    1986   "Algunos Determinantes y Principales
            Transformaciones Recientes de la Migracion
            Guatemalteca a la Frontera Sur de Mexico."
            Estudios Sociales Centroamericaonos.   Revista de
            la Secretaria General del CSUCA. No. 40 (Enero -
            Abril).

Chambers, Robert
    1982   "Rural Refugees in Africa: Past Experience, Future
            Pointers." Disasters 6:21-30.

Cipolla, Charles
    1983   "Demographic Evidence of Resistance to Changing
              Health Practices in South America." In Morgan,
              ed., Third World Medicine and Social Change, pp.
              51-68. Lanham, MD: University of Maryland Press.

Clark, Margaret
    1959   Health in a Mexican-American Culture. Berkeley:
              University of California Press.

Cosminski, Sheila
    1975   "Changing Food and Medical Beliefs and Practices
              in a Guatemalan Community." Ecology of Food and
              Nutrition 4: 183-191.

Cutts, Felicity
    1984   "Training Community Health Workers in Refugee
              Camps: A Case Study from Pakistan." Disasters
              8(3):198-205.

Davey, Ellen
    1986   "Report to the Florida Catholic Conference".
              Unpublished report.

Davis, Shelton H.
    1983   "Guatemala's Uprooted Indians: The Case for
              Political Asylum." The Global Reporter 1(3).

Delgado, Graciela, Brumback, C. L., and Mary Brice.
    1961   "Eating Patterns Among Migrant Families." Public
              Health Reports 76:349-355.

de Marcellus and Knowlton, Associates
    N.D.   Indiantown: Martin County, Florida. Indiantown,
              Florida: Indiantown Company, Inc.

DHRS
    1983   Health and Rehabilitative Services Manual. May 1,
              1983. Jacksonville: Department of Health and
              Rehabilitative Services, Florida.

Dick, Bruce and Stephanie Simmonds
    1983   "Refugee Health Care: Similar but Different."
              Disasters 7:291-303.

Durand, Mireille
    1984   "Killing Time Which Kills Us." Refugees
              (June):9-11.

Dwyer, Joanna T.
  1983   "Case Study of a National Supplemental Feeding
            Program: The WIC Program in the United States."
            In Barbara Underwood, ed., Nutritional
            Intervention Strategies in National Development.
            New York: Academic Press.

Early, John C.
  1982   The Demographic Structure and Evolution of a
            Peasant System: The Guatemalan Population. Boca
            Raton, Florida: University Presses of Florida.

Erasmus, Charles J.
  1952   "Changing Folk Beliefs and the Relativity of
            Empirical Knowledge." Southwest Journal of
            Anthropology 8:411-428.

Flores, Anselmo Mariano
  1967   "The Indian Population and its Identification." In
            M. Nash, ed., Handbook of Middle American Indians,
            Vol. 6, pp. 12-25. Austin: University of Texas
            Press.

Foster, George
  1982   "Community Development and Primary Health Care:
            Their Conceptual Similarities." Medical
            Anthropology (Summer):183-195.

Foster, George and B. Anderson
  1978   Medical Anthropology. New York: John Wiliey.

Gonzalez, Nancie S.
  1964   "Beliefs and Practices Concerning Medicine and
            Nutrition Among Lower-Class Urban Guatemalans."
            American Journal of Public Health 54 (10):
            1726-1734.

Hanlon, John J. and George Pickett
  1984   Public Health Administration. Nineth Edition. New
            York: C. V. Mosby.

Hauser, Steven
  1981   "Physician-Patient Relationships." In, E. Mishler,
            ed., The Social Contexts of Health, Illness and
            Patient Care, pp.104-140. Cambridge: Harvard
            University Press.

Holt, John
  1981   "Camps as Communities." Disasters 5:176-179.

Jelliffe, D. B. and G. J. Bennett
    1962   "Cultural Problems in Technological Assistance."
            Children 9(15):171-177.

Kaufman, Mildred
    1973   Families of the Fields, their Food and the Health.
            Report on the Florida Migrant Nutrition Project.
            Jacksonville: Florida Division of Health.

Klein, Norman
    1976   Health and Community: A Rural American Study.
            Dubuque, Iowa: Kendal/Hunt Publishing Company.

Koos, E. L.
    1957   They Follow the Sun. Florida State Board of
            Health. Monograph Number 1.

Landy, David
    1974   "Role Adaptation: Traditional Curers Under the
            Impact of Western Medicine." American Ethnologist
            1:103-127.

Logan, Michael
    1973a   "Humoral Medicine in Guatemala and Peasant
            Acceptance of Modern Medicine." Human
            Organization 32(4):385-395.

    1973b   "Digestive Disorders and Plant Medicinals in
            Highland Guatemala." Anthropos 68:538-547.

Low, Setha
    1983   "Patient Satisfaction in Costa Rica: A Comparative
            Study." In E. Morgan, ed., Third World Medicine
            and Social Change, pp.125-140. Lanham, MD:
            University of Maryland Press.

Madsen, William
    1964   Mexican Americans of South Texas. New York: Holt,
            Rinehart and Winston.

Mata, Leonardo J..
    1978   The Children of Santa Maria Cauque: A Prospective
            Field Study of Health and Growth.   Cambridge:
            Massachusetts Institute of Technology Press.

McCullough, John M.
    1973   "Human Ecology, Heat Adaptation, and Belief
            Systems: The Hot-Cold Syndrome of Yucatan."
            Journal of Anthropological Research 29:32-35.

McKinlay, John B.
   1975   "The Help Seeking Behavior of the Poor." In J.
           Kosa and I. K. Zola, eds. Poverty and Health.
           Second edition, pp.224-273. Cambridge: Harvard
           University Press.

Meredith, William and Sheran Cramer
   1982   "Hmong Refugees in Nebraska." In Bruce Downing
           and Douglas Olney, eds., The Hmong in the West.
           Southeast Asia Refugee Studies Project. Center for
           Urban and Regional Affairs. University of
           Minnesota.

Milio, N.
   1967   "Values, Social Class and Community Health
           Services." Nursing Research 16:26-39.

Miralles, Maria Andrea
   1985   "Some Observations of the Food Habits of
           Guatemalan Refugees in Indiantown, Florida."
           Unpublished report presented to the Martin County
           Health Department, Florida.

Mustian, R. David
   1980   Synthesis: Rural Health Care. Rural Development
           Series No. 10. Southern Rural Development Center,
           Mississippi State University.

Nash, June
   1970   In the Eyes of the Ancestors: Belief and Behavior
           in a Maya Community. Prospect Heights, Illinois:
           Waveland Press.

OAS
   1983   "Report on the Situation of Human Rights in the
           Republic of Guatemala." OEA/Ser.L/V/ II.61. Doc.
           47 rev.1 (Oct. 5, 1983). Washington, D.C.: General
           Secretariat of the Organization of American
           States.

Orellana, Sandra
   1977   "Aboriginal Medicine in Highland Guatemala."
           Medical Anthopology 1:113-156.

PAHO
   1984   Community Participation in Health and Development
           in the Americas. Pan American Health Organization
           Scientific Publication No. 473.

Paul, Benjamin
    1963   "Anthropological Perspectives on Medicine and
            Public Health." The Annals 346 (March), pp. 34-43.

Paul, Benjamin (ed.)
    1955   Health, Culture and Community. New York: Russel
            Sage Publication.

Press, Irwin
    1969   "Urban Illness: Physicians, Curers and Dual Use in
            Bogota." Journal of Health and Social Behavior
            10:209-218.

Reynolds, R. C., S. A. Banks, and A. Murphree (eds.)
    1976   The Health of a Rural County: Perspectives and
            Problems. Gainesville: University of Florida
            Press.

Romanucci-Scwhartz, Lola
    1969   "The Hierarchy of Resort in Curative Practices:
            the Admiralty Islander, Melanesia." Journal of
            Health and Social Behavior 10:201-209.

Rubel, Arthur
    1966   Across the Tracks: Mexican Americans in a Texas
            City. Austin: University of Texas Press.

Scrimshaw, Susan
    1978   "Stages in Women's Lives and Reproductive
            Decison-Making in Latin America." Medical
            Anthropology 2:41-58.

Scrimshaw, Susan and Elizabeth Burleigh
    1978   "The Potential for the Integration of Indigenous
            and Western Medicines in Latin America and
            Hispanic Populations in the United States." In
            Boris Veliminovic, ed., Modern Medicine in the the
            United States-Mexican Boarder Population, pp.
            31-43. PAHO Scientific Publication 359.

Shenkin, Bryan
    1974   Health Care for Migrant Workers: Policies and
            Politics. Cambridge, Mass.: Ballenger Publishers.

Shultz, George
    1986   Proposed Refugee Admissions for FY 1987. Current
            Policy, No. 866. Washington, D.C.: United States
            Department of State. Bureau of Public Affairs.

Simmonds, S., P. Vaugh, and S. Gunn (eds.)
    1983   Refugee Community Health Care. Oxford: Oxford
            University Press.

Stein, Stanley J., and Barbara H. Stein
    1970   The Colonial Heritage of Latin America. New York:
            Oxford University Press.

Tedlock, Barbara
    1982   Time and the Highland Maya. Albuquerque, New
            Mexico: University of New Mexico Press.

Underwood, Barbara
    1983   "Success or Failure of Supplementary Feeding
            Programs as a Nutritional Intervention." In
            Barbara Underwood, ed. Nutritional Intervention
            Strategies in National Development. New York:
            Academic Press.

UNHCR
    1979   Collection of International Instruments Concerning
            Refugees. Geneva: Office of the United Nations
            High Commissioner for Refugees.

UNHCR
    1982   Handbook for Emergencies. Geneva: United Nations
            High Commissioner for Refugees.

United States Bureau of Census
    1980   Indiantown, Florida (Enumeration Districts 96 and
            97), Tables 2, 3, 69, 70, 74, 91.

USDHEW
    1977   Baselines for Setting Health Goals and Standards.
            United States Department of Health Education and
            Welfare Publication No. (HRA) 77-640 (Revised
            January, 1977).

Wagley, Charles
    1967   "Mayans of Northwestern Guatemala." In Manning
            Nash, ed., Handbook of Middle American Indians,
            Vol. 6. Austin: University of Texas Press.

Washam, Robert
    1984   Letter from R. Washam, Environemntal Health
            Supervisor, Department of Health and
            Rehabilitative Services, Martin County Unit, to
            Joseph Banfi, Community Development Director,
            December 20, 1984.

Washam, Robert and Susanne Simms
   1985   "Report on the Community Block Survey of the
             Booker Park Area." (July 17, 1985). Martin County
             Public Health Unit: Florida Department of Health
             and Rehabilitative Services.

Wax, Murray L.
   1970   "Sociology." In, Otto von Mering and Leonard
             Kasdan, eds., Anthropology and the Behavioral and
             Health Sciences, pp. 39-61. Pittsburgh:
             University of Pittsburgh Press.

Weidman, Hazel.
   1979   "Falling Out: A Diagnostic Treatment Problem
             Viewed From a Transcultural Perspective." Social
             Science and Medicine 13B:95.

Winslow, C. E.
   1980   The Conquest of Epidemic Disease: A Chapter in the
             History of Ideas. Madison, WI: University of
             Wisconsin Press.

Wolf, Eric
   1959   Sons of the Shaking Earth. Chicago: University
             Chicago Press.

Woods, Clyde
   1970   "Alternative Curing Strategies in a Changing
             Medical Situation." Medical Anthropology 3:26-54.

York, S., and K. Grant
   1980   Afghan Refugees in Pakistan: A Report on Current
             Conditions. London: International Disaster
             Institute.

Young, James C.
   1980   "A Model of Illness Treatment Decisions in a
             Tarascan Town." American Ethnologist 7:106-131.

INDEX